ERRATA.

Page ix, 9th line from top, *for* "sun-dawn," *read* sun-down.
" 27, 11th " " " "and swinging arms," *read* with swinging arms.
" 55, 4th " bottom, *for* "tune and hark," *read* turn and hark.
" 84, 4th " " " "worbs," " words.
" 104, 3d " " " "furrow's," *read* furrowed.
" 110, 4th " top, *for* "whinings," *read* whirrings.
" 117, 12th " " " "valley," " valleys.
" 129, 1st " " " "master's," " muster's.
" 225, 4th " bottom, *for* "on," " no.
" 225, 5th " " " "on," " no.

Whitechurch.

Yours Ever

T. Buchanan Read

THE

NEW PASTORAL.

BY

THOMAS BUCHANAN READ.

PHILADELPHIA:
PARRY & M'MILLAN,
SUCCESSORS TO A. HART.
1855.

PHILADELPHIA:
STEREOTYPED BY GEORGE CHARLES.
PRINTED BY T. K. & P. G. COLLINS.

TO

A GROUP OF GENEROUS FRIENDS

IN PHILADELPHIA,

WITHOUT WHOSE ENCOURAGEMENT

THESE PAGES MIGHT NEVER HAVE BEEN WRITTEN,

THIS VOLUME, WITH GRATEFUL FEELINGS,

IS DEDICATED

BY

THE AUTHOR.

Florence, August 5th, 1854.

INTRODUCTION.

IF from this oaten pipe—
Plucked from the shadow of primeval woods,
And waked to changeful numbers by strange airs,
Born by my native stream, in leafy depths
Of unfrequented glades—somewhat of song
Pour through its simple stops, and wake again
In other hearts what I have felt in mine,
Then not in vain I hold it to my lips,
And breathe the fulness of my soul away.
My theme, the country—worthier theme is not
In all the tomes which star the centuries,
From blind Mæonides to Milton blind!
Oh! would that I, with all my living sight,
Might see the least of what their blank orbs saw;
And seeing, wake but once their kindling note,
And, unappalled, attempt their solemn bass;
Then would the song behind the argument
Halt at less distance. As it is, I sing,

Conscious of the disparity, and tremble, —
As who might not? But what mine eyes have seen,
Ears heard, heart felt, my muse shall teach in numbers;
Not with a bondmaid's hand, but housewife's care,
Who holds chaste plenty better than rich waste.
And not of wars terrestrial or of heaven,
Or of a hero, whose great name ablaze
With glory lights the annals of an era,
My pipe proclaims; but of that pastoral phase,
Where man is native to his sphere, which shows
The simple light of nature, fresh from God! —
That middle life, between the hut and palace,
'Twixt squalid ignorance and splendid vice; —
Above, by many roods of moral moves,
The Indian's want, and happily below —
If the superior may be called below —
The purple and fine linen; — the broad plain,
Where rests the base of our protecting walls,
Where many labour, though but few take note,
And prop the world, as pillars prop a dome.
Of trial and of triumph is my song,
Of maidens fair and matronhood sublime,
Of iron men who build the golden future, —
Heroic wills, by which the hugest oak
Is broken like a sapling; and to which
The wilderness, the rank and noxious swamps,
Inhospitable hills, renouncing all
The incumbrances of ages, bow and bear
The burthen of the harvest. — This my song.
Scorn not the muse, because mid scenes like these
She loves to wander; and, with calm delight,
Prefers to dwell among the rustic homes,
Where sweet Content, beside the well-swept hearth,
Sits like an angel, and will not depart.

To this the plush and curtains of the proud,
The stucco and thin gilding of the town—
In halls where Luxury, excited, sees
A thousand repetitions of herself
Caught into shadowy corridors, afar,
Of glass in glass interminably lost—
Were cold and naked as the winter-shed,
Through which the snow falls filtered to the floor,
Piling the cheerless drift. Let me but look
On Nature through the tranquil change of day—
The common shade and sunshine—and on life
Which, unambitious, seeks no other hues
To show her fair, or hide deformities.
Ye who would seek for aught, beside such light
And beauty as is found in summer fields,—
For theories new, where splendid errours shine,
And charm like syrens, while they drown the soul,—
For aught of song which, covertly, dispreads
The seeds which shall breed poison in the dews.
And round the foot of our great sheltering tree,
Give root to vines, with odours breathing bane,—
For any mystery deeper than which lies
Between the bounds of human wo and bliss,—
May close these harmless pages and pass on:
The truths I seek lie round us in the sun.
There are whom neither sun nor shade delights—
One warming not, the other is not grateful;
Who rest so deeply dungeoned in themselves,
No sound can waken, and no light attract;
Who lay approving hands on Nature's head,
Too wise to sit, recipient, at her feet:
The applause of such lies not within the pale
Of my ambition. Though my song may be
The transient music of a spring-time runnel,

Which may not last the season through; — or though
My light be only as an evening-taper
Placed in the casement of a hill-side home,
Which, ere the midnight, in the socket dies; —
Still will I hold the satisfying trust,
That some there are who, in a transient brook,
Can find a music which may give them joy;
Or pleasure in the taper, lit at eve
To send its ray aslant the peaceful vale.
And yet one higher hope still lights my toil,
And cheers the darkness when the lamp grows dim;
And I have pledged me in the heart to fill
The compass of this wish, if in me lies
Strength, native and achieved — and heaven vouchsafe
What else is needful, equal to the task!—
Let me but place one stone within the wall —
While the stout masons, with great plumb and line,
Are laying the foundations, broad and deep,
Of native mind, to be a temple, and
A future tower of strength, — let me but place
One stone within the wall, where worthier are,
Inscribed with Poesy! — no other word!
Whether the name of him who placed it there
Go with it, is but little; and should be,
In the just balance of true poets, — naught!

PRELUDE.

A VISION strode before me toward the west,
What time the day let drop its golden shield—
A giant form with sun-illumined face:
His hue was like the last dull bar that falls
At eve athwart the hill-tops. From his brow,
A plume of many colours 'gainst the sky
Blazed like a torch-flame. In his tawny hand
A mighty bow he bore—so tall, its top
Flamed in the sun-dawn, while the low extreme
Trailed the dusk dew, unseen, along the vale.
His eyes were deep, cavernous, unsubdued—
So deep, a curse seemed crouching in their depth—
And bent with fixed and melancholy stare;
The sun a target to his arrowy sight.
He took no note of where his footsteps fell—
No sound of tread, no rustle in the grass
Ran herald to his coming—all was soft
And noiseless as the owlet's wing. His lips

Were set in uncomplaining firmness; his right hand
Grasped, as with joy, the trophies at his girdle.
From his huge breast no word of sadness broke—
Not even a sigh to startle the calm hour!
And yet not voiceless was the air; small sounds,
Faint murmurs, delicate whisperings and low songs—
The cadence of invisible choirs, perchance,
Of aboriginal elves, which fly the haunts
Of pallid Saxons as a child a ghost;—
A choral sorrow, as if leaves and flowers,
The sprites of wood and stream and water-fall,
Were pouring out a burthen of despair,
Filling the ear of twilight, rose and rose,
Thrilled to the faint stars brightening overhead,
And fell and fell, until the deep lake heard
The shy nymphs answering from their caves forlorn.

CHORUS.

I.

O, mighty spirit, flying, ever flying!
  We are the woodlands—hearken to our wail!
Our poplars trembling and our maples sighing,
  Our great oaks bowing, as before a gale,
Our pines all sorrowing and our aspens dying,
  Our sycamores with terror growing pale,
All mourn thy flight. Oh! turn to their embraces,
Nor let the sunshine gloat upon their vacant places!

II.

O, mighty spirit, speeding, ever speeding!
  We are the hills and valleys thou hast loved!
Here rest your sires, their dead hearts freshly bleeding
  Beneath thy flight, while they lie unremoved!

Above their shrines dull foreign herds are feeding,
  And glides the grating ploughshare unreproved.
Oh! turn again—repel the foe's advance—
Rebuild your midnight fires, and weave your warlike dance!

III.

O, mighty spirit, fading, ever fading!
  We are the springs and brooklets, rivers, lakes!—
We miss your maidens—miss your children wading
  Along our sands and pebbles; and where breaks
Our lightest ripple now, it dies upbraiding
  The lonely marge, and every fountain aches!
Your light canoes lie warping on the shore,
Half-buried in the sand! Oh! turn to us once more!

CHORUS OF ALL.

O, mighty spirit, flying, ever flying!
  Thou wilt not stay and on us smile again:
Our hopes are ashes, and our hearts are dying,
  Our garlands are transmuted to a chain;
Our necks beneath the conquerors are lying,
  The toiling yoke succeeds thy peaceful reign!
The clouds have ta'en thee! We have looked our last,
And mournful memory now alone can bring the past.

The song was ended and the shade was gone,
Lost in the fiery forests of the sun.
But often since, as Eve her mantle drew
O'er her chaste bosom, stepping from her cave,
Where all the day she nods above her urn
Of dews and perfume, sentried by her owl—
The muse has watched in the departing west
Mid visionary landscapes, rivers, lakes,

O'er purple prairies, and through golden woods,
This flying shadow with his blazing bow
And flashing arrows, flaming as they flew,
Chasing the deer whose antlers mid the stars
Flung up the lustre of the dying day;
Or o'er the fallen bison saw him stand,
His red foot glowing in its gorgeous mane.
Such was the vision and its flight: and when
All this had passed — the shadow and the song —
A lovelier music to the spiritual ear
Swelled through the starry air and filled the vale, —
Sounds which seemed born in heaven, and poured
From out the constellations in the East.
Scarce sweeter were the melodies, methinks,
Heard by the shepherds on far Bethlehem's plain;
What time the flocks, waked by the midnight dawn,
Greeting the fancied advent of the day,
Arose, their fleeces dripping fresh with dew,
And cropt the wet grass in the amber light
Of that one star which ushered in a morn
That circles all the years, and, brightening, sheds
Its radiance through the ages.

CHORUS OF SPIRITS.

FIRST SPIRIT.

I am the fairest spirit breathed from God —
Not mine the praise, but His —
And where my foot-prints sanctify the sod
There peaceful plenty is.
Hail, happy land! your ancient night is through —
Receive us and be blest!
From this celestial urn of holy dew
I here baptize the West!

SECOND SPIRIT.

I am the child of her whose voice but now
  Made musical the air;
I bring the laurel which shall bind your brow,
  I come to place it there.
I bring the sword so tempered in the glow
  Of courage, truth, and right,
Its keen edge severs at one steady blow
  The tyrant's chain of might!
Unsheathed still let it gleam athwart the land,
  The light of peace or ire;
Its flash shall be as lightning in your hand —
  Its stroke, a bolt of fire!
I bring the buds of future centuries
  To bloom upon your breast —
They hold the dews of Freedom — and with these
  I here baptize the West!

THIRD SPIRIT.

I am that spirit born in Paradise,
  When man's first parents erred,
And the deep judgment thundered from the skies
  The dread commanding word.
I walked with them through far and thorny lands,
  In desert realms unknown,
And taught them toil, until their tender hands
  Were tawny as my own.
I bring the axe, the sickle, and the plow,
  Whose use alone gives rest —
And with the dews which fell from Adam's brow,
  I here baptize the West!

2

FOURTH SPIRIT.

I am that spirit who, in ages gone,
  No certain shelter found;
But here, at last, I hail the peaceful dawn,
  And bless the sacred ground.
Mine was the name the joyous angels sung,
  To cheer the shepherd's ear;
And with that Star I into being sprung,
  And with that Star am here.
And with this palm-branch, plucked from off the stem
  Of Heaven's own tree of rest,
And dipped in dews which fell o'er Bethlehem,
  I, too, baptize the West!

The chorus died; and presently the sound
Of falling forests, and the woodman's blow,
Of millwheels labouring in the stream, replied,
With one loud voice, to welcome in the band:
Then all was silent as befits the night.

THE NEW PASTORAL.

BOOK FIRST.

Fair Pennsylvania! than thy midland vales,
Lying 'twixt hills of green, and bound afar
By billowy mountains rolling in the blue,
No lovelier landscape meets the traveller's eye.
There Labour sows and reaps his sure reward,
And Peace and Plenty walk amid the glow
And perfume of full garners. I have seen
In lands less free, less fair, but far more known,
The streams which flow through history and wash
The legendary shores—and cleave in twain
Old capitols and towns, dividing oft
Great empires and estates of petty kings

And princes, whose domains full many a field,
Rustling with maize along our native West,
Out-measures and might put to shame! and yet
Nor Rhine, like Bacchus crowned, and reeling through
His hills—nor Danube, marred with tyranny,
His dull waves moaning on Hungarian shores—
Nor rapid Po, his opaque waters pouring
Athwart the fairest, fruitfullest, and worst
Enslaved of European lands—nor Seine,
Winding uncertain through inconstant France—
Are half so fair as thy broad stream whose breast
Is gemmed with many isles, and whose proud name
Shall yet become among the names of rivers
A synonym of beauty—Susquehanna!
But where, fair land, thy smaller streams invite
With music among plenteous farms, I turn,
As to a parent's fond embrace, and lay,
Well pleased, my way-worn mantle by, and shed,
With grateful heart, from off my weary feet
The white dust gathered in the world's highway.
Here my young muse first learned to love and dream—
To love the simplest blossom by the road—
To dream such dreams as will not come again.
And for one hour of that unlettered time—
One hour of that wild music in the heart,

When Fancy, like the swallow's aimless wing,
Flitted eccentric through all moods of nature—
I would exchange, thrice told, this weary day.
Then were yon hills, still beautiful and blue,
Great as the Andes; and this rushy brook,
Which the light foot-board, fallen, turns aside,
A flood considerable, with noisy falls
And gulfy pools profound; and yonder stream,
The fisher wades with ease to throw his bait
Into the larger ripple, was a river
To measure Jordan by! For then my thoughts
Were full of scriptural lore, oft-heard at morn,
And in the evening heard, until the place
Became a Palestine, while o'er the hills
The blue horizon compassed all the world.

Adieu to Fancy! Let me ope the gate,
Wide as the lane it bars, and cool my feet
Along the grassy path, and turn with joy,
As erst, to yonder chapel on the hill.
Lo! the calm Sabbath sanctifies the air,
And over all, from God's uplifted hand,
The silence falls, and, like a blessing, lies
The stillness on my spirit. The sweet sounds,
Which unprohibited from Eden time till now
Have charmed alike the day of toil and rest,

Alone assail the ear, making the quiet heard,
Soothing the soul as with a psalm! Yon bird
Which soars and falls, swinging its way thro' heaven
On airy billows, and this brook which sings
The better for the obstacles opposed,
As bards have done, together with the sounds
Of lesser note, which come from these small choirs
In leafy chapels closed, make to the ear
A music lovelier than the brazen notes
Blown through the serried pillars of cathedrals.
It is the Spring time: April violets glow
In wayside nooks, close clustering into groups,
Like shy elves hiding from the traveller's eye;
The mellow air, which from the woodland comes,
Is full of perfume shed from opening buds.
There the young maple, earlier putting forth,
In memory of the past dead Autumn gleams,
And waves its purple torch; and o'er the spring,
The willow its own sprouting in the pool
Hangs watching; while the dryad in its branches
Is dreaming of the hours when that fair maid,
The child and light of yonder cot, shall come
And, kneeling, laugh above her urn to see
Her sweet face wrinkled by prophetic waters.
The plough in this broad field with upthrown share,

There left at yester sunset, lies at rest
Along the midway furrow. Here the maize
Shall rustle through the summer; while near by
Already the live grain, which 'neath the snow
Slept the white winter through, sends up its green
And whispers in the sunshine.
Lo! anon,
From hillside homes and hamlets in the vale,
One after one, in Sabbath garb arrayed,
Their mantles breathing of deep oaken drawers
And antique chests, the people throng, and take
The various pathways which converging lead
Here to this quiet shrine among the elms.
Oh, happy hour, beloved of peace and heaven!
Around, and over all, the white calm lies
Flooded with perfume and mysterious light;
So sweet, so beautiful, it seems a day
Lost out of Eden! See, where children come,
Like hopes unchecked, still running in advance,
With innocent laughter, but not over loud,
Plucking the purple violets by the way;
While from their feet the butterfly, released
But yesterday from out his winter cell,
Darts up with devious flight, and, like a wisp,
Wavers across the meadow! Happy sounds,

By happier faces followed, still approach.
What round and ruddy cheeks are there, to which
Health, like the sun, with daily welcome comes,
Leaving the impress of his glowing hand!
But suddenly their tongues to whispers low
Drop, as their eyes look wondering on the stranger,
And into decorous columns, two by two,
They file before me with shy glances cast
From shadowy brims and snowy hoods turned back,
By matron care arranged. Some in their hands
Bear the small volume—book of praise or prayer;
And some with freedom-loving feet released
Printing the dusty path, their little shoes,
For Sunday polished, carry at the side,
To be resumed at yonder stile which gains
The highway near the church. And, following, soon
The larger people come; the youths and maids
Joining their steps as chance or fancy leads;
And, after these, stout men with faces brown,
And browner hands which on the plough-helves took,
Ungloved, the last week's sunshine. At their side
The matrons with fair brows but half-way cleared
Of household cares, which, oft accomplished, still
As oft recur, monotonous, only cheered
By virtuous sense of duty and the light

Of happy children, or encouraging words
Heard at the well-served meal; or better still,
Finding approval in their own calm hearts,
Whose gentle tempers round their daily toil
Shed music and a halo else unknown.
Here following still, with reverend steps and slow,
Their garments venerable with age, and out
Of joint with modern custom, come the sires
And mothers of the country, silver-haired.
One leans upon his cane, with knotted hands,
An oak long bowed and gnarled by tempests; one
Stands upright as a winter pine. To-day
He comes not in his long surtout of drab—
The coat of many capes and sweeping skirt,
Brushing the stubble, proof to winds rheumatic—
Now laid aside until November calls,
But in the spring-time garments of the past.
See what a brow is there, where Time delights
To place the warning record of the years!
Note the calm eye, grown mild with light of wisdom!
Assisted by his arm his partner, bowed,
Walks tottering, with a palsy-shaking head,
And mumbling to herself. Perchance she dreams,
Within her hazy brain, of that bright hour,
Now buried beneath half a century,

When on the selfsame arm she proudly leaned,
And, with the blush of youth upon her cheek,
Crossed this same pasture, and, returning, heard
And answered to another name. Her hopes
Of earth have all been realized—her dreams
Have, one by one, gone floating down the past,
Like bubbles in the sun, where envious years
Have touched them into nothing, and now point
Derision at the empty places. Thus
Full many a heart grows old, and spirit bowed,
In intellectual want—a poverty
Scarce second to the need of bread! For what,
When all the joys which stir our inward life,
And wake a pleasure in the blood, are dead
Or dying at their sources, can renew
Long past enjoyment, like the power of thought
Drawn from a wisdom gleaned in fields of knowledge?
And many a life, before its time, thus wilts
And withers to the root, and to each wind,
Adverse or fair, rustles its sad complaint,
Which else should sway with music. They should store,
Like bees in summer, for their winter want,
Nor leave improvidence to clip their wings.
Not so the form she leans on: unto him
Each sight and sound of Nature is a page

Full of fresh thought and pleasing contemplation.
A man not deep in books, but in research,
Among the hidden lore which round him lies
Most practical; and all the neighbourhood
Holds him an oracle, and reverence pays,
As well they may; for he, within these bounds,
Has held the keys of knowledge many a year,
Teaching in yonder rude house in the grove.
All these are of his scholars—first to last
Have laid their little books upon his knee,
And stumbled through their lessons undismayed,
Guided with kindness; and in every heart
Is Master Ethan filially remembered.
His son, a man of mild and easy mood—
A nature far more gentle than befits
One who must struggle with a stubborn soil—
Walks hearkening to his sire's discourse. And next,
Lo, the staid matron, with emphatic step,
Whose every movement speaks her stately soul—
The undaunted mistress of her narrow realm,
With all th' amenities which goodness gives—
A woman fit for heroes to call mother!
With form less tall and full, the daughter comes,
Her blonde hair waving round her gentle brow—
A face to be remembered, and, methinks,

Not easily forgotten; for that eye,
So deep and blue, where starry truth abides,
As in the fabled well, once on your own
Falling, with its miraculous pure light,
Stays not upon the face, but to the heart
Looks in, as through a casement, and the soul
Then feels as if an angel, going by,
Had glanced, and left its smile in passing!
And should your feet e'er wander to these vales,
The farms of Hazel-meadow, many a tongue
This picture shall attest, and, as they speak,
Mark if the sigh comes not with confirmation.
For there are hearts to which that face hath grown
A part and a necessity, as grows
A child unto the sunshine of a household;
And oft the neighbouring groves shall hear her name,
As some lone peasant takes his woodland way,
Recalling the bright summers of the past.
"Olivia!" they'll sigh, with slackened pace,
And all the leaves reply "Olivia!"
Yet unattended by the swains gallant,
Nor yet free mingling with the joyous groups
Of neighbour-maidens, from her childhood known,
She keeps her Sabbath way; still cheerful, though
Her eyes are now more kin to tears than smiles.

Nor are cold glances, sidelong looks unkind,
And jealous hate, accusing her of pride,
From former playmates cast upon her now;
But words all gentleness, and eyes all love,
Meet her where'er she turns, which kindly say,
If not in language, in each tone and act,
"We know, dear friend, the secret which you keep,
And whence the fountain of that springing tear
The smile not wholly hides. We know the pain
Which cankers at that rose upon your cheek.
We also grieve the absence which you grieve,
And mourn the distance 'twixt his heart and ours,
And pray for his return. Ships come and go,
The sea gives up its living, day by day,
And presently our Arthur shall return,
Full of brave life and wisdom—shall return,
Glowing with noble thoughts and filled with hope,
The promise of great actions. Then, beneath
The summer shade, or by the blazing hearth,
His voice shall cheer the noonday or the eve,
Recounting, with accustomed eloquence,
Rare tales of travel, intermixed with song."
Such is the comfort in each look and word
Which soothes awhile her fancy, but not long;
For absence is a shadow which no light

Can utterly dispel—a prison door,
Before the spirit, made of grated bars,
Through which the brightest day can only send
A checkered sunshine. Here next, following, come
The happy members of the parson's household;
And last, with thoughtful care conning, perchance,
The plain, unwritten sermon of the day,
The parson walks, a man of fifty years,
Who half his life has laboured in this field,
Baptizing, marrying,—and burying oft
Where death had put asunder. His broad brow
The quiet storehouse is of wisdom, learned
From open nature, and vouchsafed from God.
All week he tends within his noisy mill,[1]
Whose wheel now hangs and dreams o'er yonder
stream,
And bends his brawny shoulders to the sacks
Which daily cross the threshold; or among
The ceaseless jar and whirr of rumbling stones,
And clattering hoppers, garrulous with grain,
He walks amid the misty meal, and plans
The solemn lesson for the coming Sabbath.
His heart is full of boundless sympathies:
The stranger and the friend, the erring or
The good, come not within his genial voice

Or smile, but they go hence with firm resolve
For happy change, or strengthened in the right.
The old or young, departing, bear away
The influence of his spirit in their hearts,
E'en as they bear the mill-dust on their garments.
The sire of Arthur he, the youth who now
Wanders in foreign lands, by romance led,
Bearing the hearts and hopes of many hence;
But chiefly hers, long deemed by all his choice.

By various ways the people still come in:
Here on the hillside path, and swinging arms,
Weaving the air with visionary shuttles,
Gaunt Bowman mounts, ascending as on treadles—
Bowman, chief weaver of the vale; his wife
Close following, like himself, arrayed in suit
Of homemade russet. Down the dusty road
The vehicles, of various forms, approach:
The rattling wagon, out of joint and loose,
With temporary seats, and difficult
For unaccustomed riders; and the chaise
With rocking motion, easy as a chair,
Drawn by a jogging steed whose shoulders still
Feel the fresh record of the yester plough.
Some, rudely mounted as equestrians, come;
The switch held upward, like a sword; the horse,

With swinging head, blowing the foam in air:
And here, anon, the family steed is seen
Bearing a double burthen with slow pace.
How all the landscape, with the Sabbath scene,
Smiles with a bland and staid propriety!
About the chapel door, in easy groups,
The rustic people wait. Some trim the switch,
While some prognosticate of harvests full,
Or shake the dubious head, with arguments
Based on the winter's frequent snow and thaw,
The heavy rains, and sudden frosts severe.
Some, happily but few, deal scandal out,
With look askance pointing their victim. These
Are the rank tares in every field of grain—
These are the nettles stinging unaware—
The briers which wound and trip unheeding feet—
The noxious vines, growing in every grove!
Their touch is deadly, and their passing breath
Poison most venomous! Such have I known—
As who has not?—and suffered by the contact.
Of these the husbandman takes certain note,
And in the proper season disinters
Their baneful roots; and, to the sun exposed,
The killing light of truth, leaves them to pine
And perish in the noonday! 'Gainst a tree,

With strong arms folded o'er a giant chest,
Stands Barton, to the neighbourhood chief smith;
His coat, unused to aught save Sunday wear,
Grown too oppressive by the morning walk,
Hangs on the drooping branch: so stands he oft
Beside the open door, what time the share
Is whitening at the roaring bellows' mouth.
There, too, the wheelwright—he, the magistrate—
In small communities a man of mark—
Stands with the smith, and holds such argument
As the unlettered but observing can;
Their theme some knot of scripture hard to solve.
And 'gainst the neighbouring bars two others fan,
Less fit the sacred hour, discussion hot
Of politics; a topic, which inflamed,
Knows no propriety of time or place.
There Oakes, the cooper, with rough brawny hand,
Descants at large, and, with a noisy ardour,
Rattles around his theme as round a cask;
While Hanson, heavy browed, with shoulders bent,
Bent with great lifting of huge stones—for he
A mason and famed builder is—replies
With tongue as sharp and dexterous as his trowel,
And sentences which like his hammer fall,
Bringing the flinty fire at every blow!

But soon the approaching parson ends in peace
The wordy combat, and all turn within.
Awhile rough shoes, some with discordant creak,
And voices clearing for the psalm, disturb
The sacred quiet, till, at last, the veil
Of silence wavers, settles, falls; and then
The hymn is given, and all arise and sing.
Then follows prayer, which from the pastor's heart
Flows unpretending, with few words devout
Of humble thanks and askings; not, with lungs
Stentorian, assaulting heaven's high wall,
Compelling grace by virtue of a siege!
This done, with loving care he scans his flock,
And opes the sacred volume at the text.
Wide is his brow, and full of honest thought—
Love his vocation, truth is all his stock.
With these he strives to guide, and not perplex
With words sublime and empty, ringing oft
Most musically hollow. All his facts
Are simple, broad, sufficient for a world!
He knows them well, teaching but what he knows.
He never strides through metaphysic mists,
Or takes false greatness because seen through fogs;
Nor leads 'mid brambles of thick argument
Till all admire the wit which brings them through;

Nor e'er essays, in sermon or in prayer,
To share the hearer's thought; nor strives to make
The smallest of his congregation lose
One glimpse of heaven, to cast it on the priest.
Such simple course, in these ambitious times,
Were worthy imitation; in these days,
When brazen tinsel bears the palm from worth,
And trick and pertness take the sacred desk;
Or some coarse thund'rer, armed with doctrines new,
Aims at our faith a blow to fell an ox—
Swinging his sledge, regardless where it strikes,
Or what demolishes—well pleased to win
By either blows or noise!—A modern seer,
Crying destruction! and, to prove it true,
Walking abroad, for demolition armed,
And boldly levelling where he cannot build!

The service done, the congregation rise,
And with a freshness glowing in their hearts,
And quiet strength, the benison of prayer,
And wholesome admonition, hence depart.
Some, loath to go, within the graveyard loiter,
Walking among the mounds, or on the tombs,
Hanging, like pictured grief beneath a willow,
Bathing the inscriptions with their tears; or here,
Finding the earliest violet, like a drop

Of heaven's anointing blue upon the dead,
Bless it with mournful pleasure; or, perchance,
With careful hands, recall the wandering vine,
And teach it where to creep, and where to bear
Its future epitaph of flowers. And there,
Each with a separate grief, and some with tears,
Ponder the sculptured lines of consolation.

"The chrysalis is here—the soul is flown,
And waits thee in the gardens of the blest!"
"The nest is cold and empty, but the bird
Sings with its loving mates in Paradise!"
"Our hope was planted here—it blooms in heaven!"
"She walks the azure field, 'mid dews of bliss,
While 'mong the thorns our feet still bleed in this!"
"This was the fountain, but the sands are dry—
The waters have exhaled into the sky!"
"The listening Shepherd heard a voice forlorn,
And found the lamb, by thorns and brambles torn,
And placed it in his breast! Then wherefore mourn?"

Such are the various lines; and, while they read,
Methinks I hear sweet voices in the air,
And winnowing of soft, invisible wings,
The whisperings of angels breathing peace!

BOOK SECOND.

WHERE now Olivia, joined by her one friend
And confidant, Amy, the wheelwright's daughter,
Turns from the church, a youth from yonder town,
The village of the vale, the postman's son,
With courteous greeting, unobserved bestows
A missive blurred with foreign stamps, through which
The cyphers of her name are dimly seen.
Swift darts the flush across her cheek and brow;
Her brain is reeling with the sudden joy;
She clasps the letter as 'twere Arthur's hand,
Then slips it in her bosom, where it hears
The impatient fluttering of her happy heart.
    Both silently pursue their homeward walk,
With arm affectionate at each other's waist.
No lovelier picture e'er shall bless the vale
Than those two maidens strolling down the fields,

Their faces beautiful with various thoughts;
One lost 'mid visions rising in her soul,
Until her eyes grow dreamy with love's dew;
The other, with warm pressure of the arm,
And tender looks, pronouncing sympathy!
Their pleasing pathway leads by yonder grove;
But scarce their footsteps skirt the silent wood,
When Amy, with a shudder, checks her pace;
Olivia recoils, and both stand still!
Lo! the weird dame of Oakland stops their path!
A beldame, bowed, bearing a bunch of sticks
To light her evening fire. Her shreds of hair
Floating in snowy wisps beneath her hood,
The toothless visage, shrivelled, pinched and cramped
By years which well nigh span a century's gap,
Make her, to youthful eyes, a sight uncouth;
And even the whisper of her name oft sends
An ugly phantom to the urchin's pillow,
Smoothing his wry face in the covers hid.
Her voice is like the creak of withered limbs!
And, with a smile across her frosty face,
She summons the half timid maids approach.
Lo! there the living allegory stands
Of Winter beckoning to young May and June!
"Hey-day! fair lasses, I've a word for you!"

She cries, and holds her shrivelled finger up.
"Can you tell why the blue bird, on yon branch,
Is singing so? Ah, silly hearts, to say
It sings for simple pleasure! Know you why
This brook, which through your fathers' meadows
flows,
Makes such sweet music and so swiftly runs?
Ah, no; you have not pondered on it well.
The blue bird is a young man's heart, forsooth;
The brook, the heedless fancies of a maiden.
One sings, with all its art, to win a mate;
The other hurries, without knowing why,
Until it meets the rivers. There—go! go!
And when your sweethearts next shall clasp your
hands,
Ask them, in autumn, whither fly the birds?—
If they depart in singing pairs together?
And tell them how the winter shall come in,
And choke the brook with ice till it is dumb!
Yet, stay! you are, I see, the wheelwright's daughter
What doth he with the chips about his door,
That a poor soul is not allowed to have
A shaving but to light her faggots with?
Who grudgeth splinters may, himself, want logs;
Who gives no drink, may have his well go dry!

The kind man's wheat is seldom trampled down,
Nor oft his fence-rails feed the poor man's oven;
His herds come home, not worried by the dogs;
His horse, astray, is not put into pound!
When you are married, teach your husband this,
If you would have him thrive. But, mark you, first;
Beware the brightness of your coal black eye,
For it may fascinate to your own harm!
I have a parable for you:

A little bird there was would sing,
Would sing with all its throat,
And sang so loud that every wing
Came hurrying to the note.
A sailing hawk, among the rest,
On spotted pinions came,
And floated east, and floated west,
Still circling near his game,
Until she fancied every breast
Must feel an envious flame!

His eye was on the silly bird,
It made her heart rejoice;
She thought, too true, the great hawk heard,
With deep delight, her voice.

And, nearer still, she saw him stoop,
  On wheeling pinions gay—
The noblest wing, of all the troop,
  She fancied his that day—
Till, with one sudden, cruel swoop,
  He bore her far away!

Your sky now shines as bright as this o'er head,
But I can see, as over yon blue hills,
The white clouds rising which, before the night,
Shall fill the land with thunder and with rain."
Thus speaking with a frown, she clears her brow,
And to the other turns:—"And you, I see,
Are daughter to good neighbour Baldwin here.
You have a lover—ay, I know it well—
I rocked his cradle when he was a child,
And promised him a sweetheart fair and kind;
And as I said, a sweetheart, how he laughed,
And clapped his dimpled hands, as if the word
He could not comprehend, had music in't.
And, then, upon the day that you were born,
I took you, in your little robes of white,
And, on a pillow, bore you to the window.
'See, there,' said I, 'your sweetheart, in the field,
Is chasing butterflies among the clover!'

And then you smiled. It may be fancy, still,
Methought, I saw you smile as you smile now!
Come to my cot, anon, if you would know
The mystery of the future — when the moon
Is in the crescent, come! And, mark you well
To view her o'er the shoulder on the right;
For she is jealous, and, viewed otherwise,
Can work you direful mischief. When you plant,
Either your hopes or flowers, oh! then beware!
Consult her pleasure, and look out the signs,
Else will they bear you thorns, and never roses
And tear the hand which planted! Call me witch,
Or what you will; but only this remember,
When evil I predict, beware — beware!"
Thus saying, she adjusts her twisted load
Of gnarled sticks, and turns into the grove,
Shaking her warning finger as she goes.
"Nay, Amy dear, mind not the snarling dame!" —
Speaks mild Olivia, comforting her friend; —
"Her brain is far more crooked than her body;
Her temper is as crabbed as a thorn,
Which, when an ill wind blows, can only chafe
And worry its own branches! Mind her not!
'Tis evident she holds a harmless grudge.
Poor soul! I needs must pity her — so old,
And so forlorn — she must be miserable!"

To which the other answers, with a shudder,
"Some say she is a witch, and can work harm,
Send sickness 'mong the cattle, and brew storms!"
"Mere superstition!" cries her friend. "'Tis wrong,
'Tis sinful, to hold such belief of one
Whom God has made, even as he has us!
The height of her pretence is but to tell
The fortune, from the hand, as many do,
Which hath no further harm in it than this,
That some there are, who, foolishly, have faith,
And wait her promises, with hope or dread.
Why, I, myself, will turn a cup, and read
The accidental figures in the grounds,
And thereby, with shrewd guesses, tell the future;
And yet I am no witch! I pity her:
And I have heard my grandsire often say,
There was a time when she was young and fair,
And light of heart, as either you or I;
And how she was betrothed, and how the war
Left her as friendless as we see her now.
Suppose—but, no, we will not think of that;
But let us pity the poor crone, and pray,
When we grow old, we may not be like her."
Thus saying, they approach diverging paths,
And, after sweet adieus, take separate ways.

BOOK THIRD.

How, o'er the silent fields, the white heat gloats
And shimmers like a silver swarm! Anon,
A distant rumbling shudders through the air,
Shed from those domes of thunder in the west,
Which swell and rise, and, brightening, as they swell,
Show the black walls beneath, from out whose ports
The flash shall lighten and the rain be poured!
The warning given, the various stragglers hear,
And note it well, and hasten to their homes.
Olivia, now, hath crossed her native porch
Where, earlier arrived, the family sit.
There, unappalled by unmolesting friends,
The russet wren glides in among the vines,
And adds another straw unto its nest,
Then, on the neighbouring trellis, pours its song.
The poor man's cottage is its favourite haunt;

And he is poor, indeed, who to his roof
Can welcome not the yearly visitor,
To cheer his door with music! There, too, comes,
But less to be desired, the boring bee
Blowing his warning horn, and in the wood
Mining his secret galleries secure.
A carpenter is he who for himself
Builds, and destroys for others; while the dust
Of his incessant saw upon the floor
Demands the busy broom. Some on the face
Wear the white badge of innocence, and these
Fall frequent captives to the boy who frights
The smaller children with the stingless shape.
The wayward swallows flicker through the air,
Or, safely sheltered 'neath the mossy eaves,
Sit chattering scandal at their clay built doors;
While others, with a taste for soot and smoke,
Dart down the chimney, with a muffled noise,
Echoing the distant thunder. For these sounds
Olivia hath no ear, nor any eye
For aught save that dear page o'er which she pores,
Reading it with her heart as with her sight
Secure from all intrusion, there she sits
Beside her chamber window. O'er the sill
The creeping vine looks in, and on her brow,

Flushed with delight, the passing air is shed
Fresh with the perfume of the coming rain;
And ere she is aware the darkness falls,
Deeper than twilight, and the first big drops
Rattle like pebbles on the sultry shingles,
And splash the window-ledge. Then bursts the
 shower,
And roars along the roof. The while, outside,
The housetop smokes with the rebounding spray;
The troughs with fulness choke and overrun;
And noisy water, streaming from the eaves,
Deepens the furrows in the earth beneath.
Or, if the shower abates a breathing spell,
The crooked flash blinds the calm instant, when
The sudden thunder stamps upon the storm,
And fiercer, fuller, louder than before,
The drowning deluge pours, and frights the house
To silence and to wonder. Still she reads,
And thus the tenor of the letter runs:—

"The lands which I most wished to tread,
 The scenes which I most wished to see,
The shrines of the immortal dead
 Have known me, and I now am free.

There is no claim the tyrant makes
  So strong as that of young Desire,
No cloud the syren Music wakes
  So sweet as Fancy's pilgrim lyre.

I've traced the chain which led me on,
  And saw it fall, like links of sand,
And followed till the charm was gone
  From Fancy's harp-awaking hand.

If for myself I lived alone,
  If there was no fond heart to greet
With love the fulness of my own,
  I here could deem my life complete.

Desire achieved is pleasure lost—
  Hope dies when cold possession comes—
And Memory poorly pays the cost
  With her exact and formal sums."

Thus far she reads, and with a tremor stops.
A tear is on the page—one mournful tear—
As it would blot the last sad verse away.
Who tells me Love is blind? Oh, say not so!
He is an Argus in the soul which sits

And watches with a hundred tireless eyes—
A diligent recorder of each act
And word is he. The steward of his house
Sleeps not in indolence beside the wine,
Or squanders among strangers, unrebuked,
The master's wealth! And still Olivia reads:—

"If I have said, a hope achieved
  Is something lost, oh! do not frown;
Nor let your gentle mind be grieved
  That love when won is pleasure flown.

For, in my inmost heart, I hold
  Our love was never here begun;
But, old as our two souls are old,
  It dates more cycles than the sun.

That somewhere, in God's outer space,
  Our spirits had together birth,
With kindred ties, no time or place
  Can utterly destroy on earth.

Then since our love was never won,
  And cannot wilt in sun or frost,
Still let me sing, as I have done—
  'Desire achieved is pleasure lost!'"

Her heart, rebuked, is touched to tenderness,
And through the starry light of swimming tears,
Too happy to be shed, she reads again:—

"Thy brightness so encircles me
  I cannot reach its bounds,
What though my footsteps daily trace
  The paths of foreign grounds?

I walk in an unbroken dream
  Of thy remembered light,
A moving dome it glows by day,
  A sheltering arch by night!
My waking hours in peace are spent—
I sleep as in a guarded tent!"

Oh, love, thrice happy love, that thus can make
A day of darkness, and, at noontime, shed
A light which gilds the sunshine! Nought she hears,
Nor sees the swelling freshet in the vale,
The streaming, roaring torrent, bearing down
Dead limbs and fallen trees, and in its wrath
Leaving the meadows fenceless, and, anon,
Robbing the woodman of his winter cords.
Still, as the rain assaults the roof, she reads:—

"I see Italia, with her spires and domes,
Her pinnacled cathedrals and her towers,
Her castles, and gray ruins, and the homes
Of splendid infamy in princely bowers!
Here Sin and Shame together herd, like gnomes
Mining in secret, and here Hunger cowers,
And squalid Want before the palace waits,
And stays the stranger passing at the gates!

Where Art, of all the good which hath been, lives
Holding decaying state, half imbecile,
Like Tyranny, and now no more receives
The aid of genius, but with fading smile
Lives on the past; or, if a new hand gives —
As Alston and Thorwaldson gave erewhile —
An impulse to her old triumphal car,
It is not native here, but comes from far!

Where once the North, in swift destruction skilled,
Trampled the arts to ruin, now, behold,
Across the Alps it comes again to build;
And the New World, with reverence for the Old,
Sends her few sons, with native ardour filled,
Lending new life where all is dead and cold.
The Tuscan capitol and haughty Rome
Grow prouder while they hold our sculptor's home.

But all these glorious galaxies of art—
  This antique world—this garden of the past—
Not long can bid the dream of home depart.
  The marble Venus hath a charm to last
With those alone who wear a wandering heart.
  Beside the Apollo, watching where is cast
His long gone arrow, oft I stand and see
Its far flight ever guiding back to thee.

Oh! for one hour along the quiet lane,
  Which leads between the school and thy dear home,
To breathe those tender April vows again!
  Or by the stream, or through the woods to roam,
As we were wont when summer held her reign,
  Conversing love, though from our lips might come
No sound of words! Oh, sighing hearts, give o'er,
Ye yet shall sing together as of yore!"

The page is finished, and a sudden glow,
Sent from an iris towering in the east,
Sheds o'er her face its lustre, till she sees
And blesses the bright bow, as happy sign
And confirmation of her lover's words!

BOOK FOURTH.

The storm is past; but still the torrent roars,
Louder and louder, with incessant swell.
The brook, near by, hath overswept its bounds,
Drowning its tallest rushes; and the board
Which made the path continuous to the school—
And where the children loitered to behold
The minnows playing—now is borne afar,
Sweeping above the bowing hazel tops.
Within the opening west, the careful sun—
Like one who throws his mansion doors apart,
And looks abroad, to scan his wide estate—
Is forth to note the progress of the storm,
And what its rage hath wrought. Afar and near,
The clouds are all ablaze with amber light;
The earth receives it, and the fields look glad;
And still the rainbow, brightening as it grows,

Rises and bends, and makes the perfect arch.
All crowd the porch, and wonder at the flood,
With various surmises and alarms;
And Master Ethan takes his hat and cane,
("Pilgrim," he calls the cane for it hath been;
Through many generations handed down,
Since first some long gone ancestor had found
The straight stem growing in an English grove
And gave the ivory top,) "Pilgrim" he takes,
And strides across the vale. Not winding round
By easy paths, but with a course direct
O'er fences and ploughed fields, to younger feet
Forbidding, bends his steps, and gains the mill;
And lo! the sad fulfilment of his fears!
The dam has burst! and, with a roar of triumph,
The freshet mocks the miller as it flies.
There stands the parson, there his good wife stands,
Surrounded by their children, and with words
Of wonder and of comfort Ethan comes.
The miller takes his sympathizing hand,
And in reply makes answer with a sigh—
"He rules the storm, the floods are in his hold,
He gives and takes, and doeth all things well!"
The sun goes down; the day departs in peace;
And through the vale the starry tapers gleam,

Signals of household calm, from cottage homes;
And here and there, perchance, the slender ray
Conducts the venturous feet of rustic swain,
Who seeks the fireside where the maiden sits
Expectant of his step and welcome knock.
Not thus Olivia waits; but even thus,
Beside the wheelwright's evening-lighted hearth,
Her gentle friend, with an uneasy breast,
Holds anxious quiet till her lover comes.
Not long she waits, but, with a fluttering heart,
Hears his approach, and welcomes him with smiles
And maiden blush discreet. The well-pleased sire
Takes, with rough grasp, the youth's smooth hand in his,
And points the place of honor by the fire.
The matron, with misgivings in her mind,
Bends the cold nod, and, bustling for a while
About her household cares, withdraws in doubt
Shaking her dubious head. Not so the squire:
He sits and lights his pipe, in social mood,
Which, oft as jovial converse lets go out,
As oft the glowing ember reillumes.
At last, with easy tapping at the jamb,
The ashes fall; the pipe is laid aside,
And he departs, and leaves the room to love;—

To happy whisperings, breathing words so low
That nought is heard except the cricket's song,
In chorus with the simmering of the log
And muttering flame, which hath a voice prophetic.
Oh, Muse, forbear! Although 'mid scenes like this,
Thy wont is ever to draw softly near,
And sit eavesdropping at the door of Love!
Forbear, forbear! and be no record kept,
Except within the pages of their hearts,
For Time hereafter to peruse with joy,
Or Grief to blot with tears. Or if to note
Thou needs must lend thine ear, approach, invade
The sanctuary, by intruding feet
Seldom assailed—chief bed-room of the house—
And say the tenor of the long dispute.
"He is no choice of mine," so speaks the spouse.
To which the squire demands, with testy words,
"A reason, wife, a reason?—without that
Your talk is but an idle wind, to which
My set conviction is no weathervane."
"Well, call it but a wind," the wife replies;
"But 'tis a wind which runs before the storm,
And tells which way the bitter cloud is coming.
And, as for reason, it is quite enough
My heart mislikes him, and I never found

My instincts wrong. Besides, you know the dream
I told you of." To which the husband answers,
With growing tartness, "Wind—heart—instinct—
dream!
A woman's reason truly! Now hear mine:
The youth is comely, and our daughter loves him,
And, fresh returned from college, is well bred,
With so much learning that the neighbourhood
Looks on him wondering, and the loutish swains
Eye him with jealousy. Who, more than I,
Should know the advantage of a well stored mind?
Hence am I magistrate; and he may be,
As he is like to be, the people's choice,
And take his seat in Congress. Then remark
What honour follows, which must e'en reach us."
To which the wife—"Were he the Governor,
I would not bate a jot what I have said.
Where goes my liking not, I ask no honour.
He is no choice of mine. You may despise
The dream I told you; but I say his eye
Is just the eye that glittered in the snake;
So like that, when he looks at me, I shudder,
And chiefly when he smiles. And he wears rings—
I like not that—the snake was also ringed."
"Tush, woman!" cries the squire, interrupting;

"Look Reason in the face, and put to blush
Your childish superstition! Answer this:
Who hath the largest farm in all the State?
Who the best cattle? Who the fullest purse?
And is not this his heir?" The spouse replies,
With bitterness which gives each sentence strength:
"How was the farm procured? Bit after bit,
By cunning tricks of law. If each had theirs—
The poor man, and the widow, and the orphan—
Those cattle would go home to different stalls.
Case after case hath come to you for trial;
And you should know—for it hath oft been said,
Oft been a taunt our children heard at school—
That you gave favour 'gainst the poor man's cause.
Oh, Walters, many a time as I have heard
Some neighbour here recount to you his wrongs,
My heart has ached, and indignation flamed,
Until I wished that, in your icy stead,
I might sit there and hold the whip of Justice!
He, too, is maker of that poison drug
Which blights the land with poverty and woe.
His still-house knows no rest, by day or night,
Until one needs must think a demon tends it.
Oh, he hath much to answer for, and grows
More fat in sin than body! E'en the swine

He yearly bloats for slaughter at his troughs,
Roll in less ugliness than he to me."
The husband, angered, scarce can find reply;
He feels the truth, but will not leave his point;
His judgment, like a wayward child rebuked,
Grows sullen and determined in the wrong,
But presently responds:—"Well, say no more;
When weds the maid, the maid shall have her choice,
And if it be this youth—so let it be."
To which the wife makes answer with resolve:—
"I shall forbid, and if against my voice,
Encouraged on by you, the girl shall go,
Then be what mischief follows at your door—
I'll none of it." The voices cease; and now
The stars of midnight glimmer o'er the vale;
The wheelwright's gate swings o'er the silent dark,
And one lone rider occupies the road.

BOOK FIFTH.

THE lamp, renewed, still sheds a cheerful light,
Hope lends a halo to its steady blaze;
And through the casement beam the westward stars,
Taking their noiseless way, and shining still,
Though sleeps the world and there are few to note.
And thus, encouraged by example high,
The Muse awakes her simple theme and sings,
And breathes, in the attentive air of night,
The song to-morrow may refuse to hear.
When comes the tumult of the noisy day,
And the great city, like a cataract, swells,
Pouring its drowning tide of toil and trade,
Not Pan's own pipe might bid it tune and hark,
And, hearkening, be refreshed,—much less the tune
Floating unskilful from these rustic stops.
Oh, thou to-morrow! wherefore wilt thou rise,

And shake the quiet from thy garment's fold,
E'en as a lion shakes the dream of peace
From out his mane, and springs upon his prey?
As on the Sabbath, birds and brooks will sing,
The flowers come forth and gentle airs shall breathe,
Laden with perfume; yet wilt thou go forth,
Girded with love of transient gain and power,
As if the world of beauty and of song
Behind the gates of yesterday lay closed!
Oh, rapid age, whence tends thy noisy course?
Thy roaring wheels affright me, and I shrink—
Shrink to the wayside hedge, and stand appalled;
And, 'mid the smoke and discord, blindly ask
The question none will spare the time to answer!
Whence tends thy course? To that white mart of Peace
Where Wisdom, on the perfect throne of Knowledge,
Reigns absolute, and Justice, loving all,
And by all loved, hath dropped her useless scales?
Or to the realm of Discord, where the walls,
For their stupendous height, shall one day fall,
With louder ruin, round the homes of men;
And this huge tower aspiring to the heavens,
Which Science daily rears, be stayed at last
With multitudinous jargon of wild tongues?

Vain question, where no voice will make reply.
Time only answers in the distant future,
So far his words faint in the midway air,
Or come in broken murmurs, like the sea's,
Dying uncomprehended. Still my soul
Holds faith in man and in his progress forth;
Since not alone 'tis his, but God's.
Day dawns,
And with it swell the sounds, afar and near,
Of lowing cattle and the crowing cocks.
From farm to farm the wakening signals run,
And the blue smoke ascends. The sheep, released,
Leap the low bars and, following their bell,
Go bleating to the pasture. And, anon,
The ploughman drives his team into the field,
And treads the furrow till the horn recalls.
Meanwhile the kine their generous udders yield,
And fill the sounding pail, till it o'erruns,
And drips the path with foam. Then, at the spring,
The snowy liquid poured in careful rows,
And on the watery slabs arranged to cool,
Gleams like a series of full moons. Afar
The giant forge, at labour 'mid the hills,
Throbs sullen thunder from its iron heart,
And 'neath yon poplar, bursting into bloom,

The lesser anvil rings. While from the cot
Which on the breezy upland greets the east,
The windows blazing with the morning red,
The loom makes answer with its busy beat.
    Look in to-day upon the murmuring school.
There sits the old man at his wonted desk,
Round which the scholars stand in crescent rows,
Class after class, the oldest coming first;
Then, gradually descending, till the child
In russet slip comes tottering to his feet,
And finds a place upon the knee of age,
Where dimpled fingers point the letters wrong,
Or stray unchided to the master's watch-seals.
How like a hive, the busy school house hums!
Till comes the hour of recess, when in streams,
With laughter loud, they pour into the air,
And join in various games. Two desks there are,
Which hold for all especial charms; and oft
The smiling children mark them out, and point
On one the deep carved "O." Six times the Spring
Hath breathed its odours round the sacred place,
Since here the boy engraved the charmed cypher;
And yearly the tradition is passed down,
"There sat Olivia, and here Arthur sat."
Now bloom the orchards, and the noisy bees

Sing like a wind among the snowy limbs.
The occupants of neighbouring garden hives
Are there, in full communities, to mine
The odorous Eldorado; and the wasp
Dropping his long legs, like a flying crane,
Lights on the flower, and, with his ready sting,
Threats the intruder. There the humble-bee
Comes booming, and departs with laden thighs.
The yellow-jacket, small and full of spite,
Bedecked in livery of golden lace,
Comes with the fretful arrogance of one
Who plays the master, though himself a slave;
And over all, the tyrant of the hour,
The kingbird, hovers, darting on his prey;
And takes the ventured argosy of sweets,[2]
Then boasts his conquest on the adjacent branch,
Where, like a pirate hauled against the wind,
He waits another sail. From limb to limb,
The birds which here delight to build their nests—
The blue-bird, and the robin, and the small
Gray wood-pecker—now flit among the flowers,
Until the air is full of life and song,
As it is full of perfume. Now begins
The housewife's happiest season of the year.
The ground, already broken by the spade—

The beds, made level by the passing rake—
The almanac consulted, and the signs
Conspiring favour—forth with apron full
Of choicest seeds, the best which last year gave,
She sallies to the garden where, all day,
Breathing the pleasant odour of the mould,
She bends and plants, while, to her eye of hope,
Here springs the early pea, and there the bean,
The lettuce and the radish, and what else
Her culinary providence requires.
But chief of all, with careful hands, she sets
The slips, and bulbs, and seeds which, round each bed,
Shall make a bright embroidery of flowers.
Thus the dame Baldwin in her garden bends.
Meanwhile, Olivia by the mellow air,
Her winter task of flax not wholly spun,
Is woo'd unto the porch, where at her wheel,
Where sat her grandma generations since,
She sits and sings, not loud but low.
The little wren to listen stops his song,
And wonders on the woodbine. Thus she sings:—

"A damsel dwelt in a mansion old,
Her eyes were blue, her hair was blonde;
The hills were bright, the sky was gold,
Where rose the flaming sun beyond.

The red stream of the rising day
  Set all her windows east a-glow,
And on her face the morning ray
  Still stole, as it were loth to go.

And there she spun the silver flax,
  But guessed not what the woof would be,
While, through her hands of snowy wax,
  The white thread ran incessantly.

As fair as any queen, in sooth,
  She toiled and held a noble trust;
Her heart had whispered this one truth—
  What work would brighten, sloth would rust.

'There is a loom,' she said, 'receives
  Whatever skeins my reel shall bear;
There is a weaver, daily weaves
  The woof which I, perforce, must wear.

And be the thread or coarse or fine,
  The loom is still the sure receiver;
Whate'er I spin, the same is mine,
  Returned in full from Time the weaver!'"

BOOK SIXTH.

Along the roads, with busy pick and spade,
The neighbours gather, and, in cheerful groups,
Repair the way. Some hold the heavy plough,
Which grates and scours along the sandy side,
Or from the rock rebounds, with sudden jerk,
Or caught beneath the deep-laid elm-root, stalls.
Some fill the gullies which the winter made,
And with broad shovels smooth the gravelly ground.
And all, with frequent jest and laugh, pursue
Their labour, making holiday of toil;
And, when the work is done, turn cheerly home,
Well pleased to know the yearly tax is paid.
Now comes the mid-week; and, from various roads,
Behold the frequent chaise, with easy jog,
Taking its tranquil way to yonder grove—
A grove of Lombard poplars, tall and saint-like—

And under which the long, low building stands,
Gray with the touches of a century,—
A house of meditation and of prayer,
The favourite temple of meek-handed Peace.
There meets the calm community of "Friends,"
The old and young, in rigid garb arrayed;
The same their grandsires wore, and, in their hope,
The same their far descendants shall put on,
Remembering their fathers, and their faith,
And simple piety. The ample brim
Shades the white patriarchal hair of age,
And the brown locks of youth. There maidenhood,
Its gay soul glancing from meek bending eyes,
Walks, like the matron, in staid habit dressed.
How beautiful, in those straight hoods of silk,
And scrupulous lawns, which shield their tender necks,
The gentle Rachels, Ruths and Deborahs pass!
There oft the Christian virtues come in name,
And oft in spirit, walking hand in hand—
Hope cheering Faith, with Charity between.
But this, alas! is fading year by year;
From out the Quaker chrysalis are born
The wings which wear the changing hues of fashion;
And feet, released, forget their ancient thrall,
And for the late constraint, with lighter tread,

Lead through the mazes of the intricate dance,
Imported fresh from foreign capitols.
Their mission is accomplished; and the march
Of this calm band, which, in the van of Peace,
Walked, conquering with forbearance, 'mid reproach,
And jeers of ridicule, is o'er; and now
The few who still surround the saintly tent,
And prop it 'mid the advancements of the time,
May rest upon the memory of the past,
Content with its results. The future comes,
And things, which have been useful in their day,
Are driven into the bygone realms of old,
And leave no vestige of their powerful camps.
The good, which they have wrought, alone survives—
The form in which it came, departs, and this
Is undistinguishably merged at last,
And in the general stream of progress lost.
New orders come, as old ones take their leave;
And "welcome" sounds not oftener than "adieu."

The streams, which late the storm had overcharged,
Have fallen, and left the record of their height
Marked on the woodland trunks; while here and there,
Where obstacles opposed, the muddy drift
Is lodged to dry, and in the summer sun
Become the rest of reptiles, and what else

In such vicinities consort. When comes
The mantled winter, this may be the haunt
Of timid rabbits, and the flocking quail;
Where oft the hunter, with his dog, shall steal
Tracking the knee-deep snow; and shivering here,
The children of the poor shall frequent come,
And tear the tangled drift apart, and bear
The frozen branch to light their dreary hearth.
The stream has fallen; and at the miller's dam,
The neighbours, by good master Ethan called,
Collecting come with crowbar, pick and spade,
And in the breach begin the swift repair.
How like a miracle the progress is
Of cheerful labour, wrought by numerous hands
Working in concert, where the heart and hand
Conspire, well pleased, to do a generous act!
No hope of recompense, which wealth can give,
Sends such alacrity to hands humane,
As doth the sense of doing noble duty.
The day which sees a liberal deed complete,
A fellow creature in misfortune helped,
Falls round the doer, at its evening close,
With gentle airs and loving dews of peace;
Sleep, like an angel, at his pillow sits,
And charms his lids 'gainst ill-intruding dreams.

6*

The week draws near its close, and now the school
Takes wonted holiday. It is a time
The older children are required at home.
The wide-mouthed oven must be set a-roar,
Fired by such light brush and broken rails
As fence and woodland yield. These bring the boys,
Dragging the crackly loads with shouts of glee.
At home the girls, delighted, tend the babe,
And teach it by the sliding chair to walk —
How beautiful to watch their loving care,
The future mother swelling in their breasts!
While those, which date nor yet so young nor old,
Beneath the orchard crowd the little swing,
Or in the barn disturb the secret nest.
Some by the roadside build the mimic house,
With moss and broken ware set out. Meanwhile
The busy matron, o'er the floury tray,
Kneads the huge loaf; or on the snowy board
Rolls the thin crust, and crimps the juicy pie.
Then, from the paddle broad, the pan and dish
Glide grating to the heated cave to bake.
By noon, the ample tables and the shelves
Groan with the weight of swollen loaves, embrowned,
And pies arranged to cool; and all the air
Is redolent with the delicious scent

Which makes the appetite by expectation,
And whets the watery tooth!

From the warm south
The whispering breezes flow; and the calm sky
Is flecked with shadowy vapours, scarcely clouds,
Through which the sun rolls lazily and red.
This master Ethan notes, and takes his rod—
For he has heard, for weeks, the whistling swamps
A welcome signal to the fisher's ear—
And, with the feeling fresh as when a youth,
Makes through the meadow, where the stream invites,
And to the surface gives the tempting bait.
And there the well-pleased grandchild bears the string—
No love of gentle Walton charms his brain;
His art is such as anglers only know
Who from experience learn to trim the hook,
And swing the whip-like line. The bait is rude;
No artificial fly, with golden wing,
Flits o'er the ripple; yet, as oft he throws,
The round chub, whirling on its watery wing,
Darts through the wave, then flutters on the land.
Above, below—they will not mar his sport—
The ploughmen, boisterous from their finished fields
With nets relentless scoop the deepest pools,
And throw the heterogeneous tribes ashore.
Some whose long task detains them through the day,

Treading the furrows, when that eve sets in,
Will come with torch and spear, and wade the stream;
Or at the rude boat's prow, beneath the blaze
Dripping with flaming pitch, with watchful eye
And steady hand direct the sure harpoon.
    Another week comes in. The Sabbath past,
The old and young are gathered to the fields.
Some walk the furrow, and let drop the maize,
With measured space between; while some, behind,
With hoe industrious conceal the grain,
And form the little mounds, erelong to sprout
And wave their rustling plumes. This done, behold,
The hideous shape is throned upon the field!
A figure built awry, with outstretched arms,
And, like a drunkard maudlin, in the wind
Flutters its rags, and frights the pilfering crow.
    Now blooms the lilac, sweetening all the air;
And by the brook the alder, and the rose,
Propt at the cottage door with careful hands,
Bursts its green bud, and looks abroad for May.
To-morrow, and the smiling month shall come.
To-morrow! what delight is in to-morrow!
What laughter and what music, breathing joy,
Float from the woods and pastures, wavering down
Dropping like echoes through the long to-day,
Where childhood waits with weary expectation!

BOOK SEVENTH.

MAY has come in — young May, the beautiful —
Wearing the sweetest chaplet of the year.
Along the eastern corridors she walks,
What time the clover rocks the earliest bee,
Her feet a-flush with sunrise, and her veil
Floating in breezy odours o'er her hair;
And ample garments, fluttering at the hem,
With pleasing rustle round her sandal shoon.
What happy voices wake the rural airs,
From hillside homes and valley cottages,
And every village is alive at dawn!
Long ere the dews have winged themselves to heaven,
In vernal paths the little bands are out,
Winning their course, with joyous steps and song,
Until the Oaklands take them to their arms,
And grove to grove, with loving voice, proclaims

The gladness which it feels. Before the sun
Hath burnt the western shadows from his dial,
Olivia and Amy through the shade
Walk in their snowy garments of the time,
O'er which the flickering sunshine, through the boughs,
Dances amid innumerous phantom leaves,
Chasing those lovely forms where'er they go,
And starring them with brightness. Arm in arm,
They print the tender mosses, and disturb
The broad-leafed mandrake, bending here and there
To pluck the violets peering through the leaves;
Or those small woodland flowers, so delicate
That fancy deems them the exotic blooms
Of fairy gardens, planted in the night,
And nurtured by the moon. With converse sweet,
And confidence which young hearts only know—
So pure themselves, they have not guessed how deep
The world is lored in treachery—they each
To each repeat the secrets of their loves.

Beneath yon whispering maple in the lawn—
A dainty lawn in middle of the woods—
The Mayday groups are gathered, and from there
The air comes laden with the breath of mirth;
And Amy and Olivia, in delight,
Withhold their steps, and gaze between the trees—

'Twixt shadowy vistas of huge mossy trunks
And drooping vines — and watch the floating forms,
Now seen, now hid, like stars 'mid broken clouds,
All wildly dancing 'neath their scented wreaths,
As they the embodied spirits were of flowers.
And presently, ascending to her throne,
One lovely maid for coronation mounts.
And thus, along the gladdened air, is borne
The song which greets her and proclaims her queen.

We bring roses, beautiful fresh roses,
  Dewy as the morning and coloured like the dawn;
Little tents of odour, where the bee reposes,
  Swooning in sweetness of the bed he dreams upon.
Roses, fresh roses from the young Spring borrowed,
  To bind round your tresses where the zephyr loves
    to play.
Smile, gentle princess, while your snowy forehead
  Takes the sweet coronal which crowns you queen
    of May!
        Roses, fresh roses,
    Which crown you queen of May!

We bring violets, the purple and the azure,
  Which bloomed at the coming of the blue bird's
    wizard wing,

To greet your dear presence they oped their eyes of pleasure,
Then bowed, and they wept that you came not first of spring.
Violets, sweet violets, we plucked from April's bosom,
The last which he smiled upon before he passed away;
And thus round your forehead shall fairy bud and blossom
Shine in the coronal which crowns you queen of May!
Violets, sweet violets,
Which crown you queen of May!

We bring daisies, little starry daisies,
The angels have planted to remind us of the sky.
When the stars have vanished they twinkle their mute praises,
Telling, in the dewy grass, of brighter fields on high.
Daisies, bright daisies, to gleam around your tresses,
Until your brow shall shine like the dawning of the day;
And thus, as the coronal your lovely forehead presses,
We bow to your sceptre, and we hail you queen of May!
Daisies, bright daisies,
Which crown you queen of May!

Thus fly the hours to youthful fancy dear.
Now, midway in the afternoon, the sun
Descends upon his poised and flaming wing,
Looking aslant the earth; and still
The voice of joy, with simple music joined,
Thrills through the grove, which not to childhood only
Yields up its vernal spaces, but to youths
And maidens, who come gaily flocking in,
And round the rustic viol reel the dance.
There trusting Amy greets a welcome hand,
And, hearkening to the voice she loves, floats down
From sun to shadow in bewildering maze.
The woods swim round, the trees with linked hands
Whirl through the music and the misty light,
With giant gesture and half human smile,
Swaying as to a wind. And thus the maid,
Clasped by the arm of love, forgets the world.
Alone Olivia strolls beyond the place,
Seeking in unfrequented paths the quiet
Her soul desires—communion with itself;
And following her heart, which fondly leads,
She finds the sacred places where, in days
Long gone, she walked with Arthur at her side.
Here was the spot where from the summer school,
When childish liking heralded their love,

They wandered, and from honeysuckle boughs
Gathered nectarean fruit. Here was the place
They walked beside the brook, and gaily plucked
The spiry rushes which, with rustic art,
They wove in little baskets; such as held
The handful of wild berries, after gleaned,
From vines which stole beneath the meadow grass,
Or at the briery fence-side grew. Here was the scene—
Dear heart be calm!—where, 'neath these sheltering
    limbs,
When the broad poplar filled his cups of gold—
Where every wandering wind and pilgrim bee
Drank, and, departing, boasted of the draught—
Her ear had caught the low first words of love,
Her hand had felt the first declaring pressure;
And now, as then, she leans against the tree.
Her hair escaping glides unto her shoulder;
From out its folds the wild flowers, like her tears,
Drip noiseless and unnoted to the ground.
The sun descends; the long and level ray
Kisses the maiden's shoulder, and glides up,
Flaming a little in the poplar's top;
Then, lighting on a fleecy cloud o'erhead,
Burns, fades and dies as embers in the ashes.

BOOK EIGHTH.

The spring departs; and, in her speeding haste,
Chased by a swarm of murmuring winds and bees,
Scatters the withered lilacs as she flees.
The blue bird mourns for her; the russet wren
Leads out its young, to see her ere she leaves.
Her hands are full of garlands, some a-bloom,
Some budding and some dead. With floating hair,
Thus fled Ophelia in her frenzied hour;
And, like Ophelia, from her willow branch,
Spring, singing, falls into the lilied pool,
And in the crystal stream of summer drowns.
The heavens a little weep above her form,
What time she floats adown into the past,
Till June, full blown and blooming, like her rose,
Comes laughing in beneath the rainbow arch.

It is the season when the stormy hive

Gives forth the noisy whirlwind of its swarm,
Which swings awhile above its ancient home,
With whirrings louder than a housewife's wheel,
And warns the dame of their intended flight;
When forth she sallies, all a-glow with fear
And anxious hope, and on the sounding pan
Beats like a maniac drummer in mid battle,
Filling the air with wild, discordant noise,
Until, for thus her rustic fancy deems,
The guiding voice of the great sov'reign bee
Is drowned amid the tumult. Then, perforce,
Their further flight is stayed; and on a limb,
With layer o'er layer, they settle till the branch
Droops with the black, impending weight; and then
The ready hive receives the living mass.
Or, if too late the ringing pan assails,
Behold the swift and winding line, afar,
Flies warping on the sun-illumined air,
And mocks the disappointed eye, until
Amid the distant forest boughs it sweeps,
And, like a veil entangling, clings and lights
Too high to be regained. Then, in some tree,
Some hollow oak, or beech, or sycamore,
Driving the astonished squirrel from his home,
They fix their habitation, and at once

Fill up their waxen garners with the sweets
The woodland blossoms and the clover yield;
And little reck how, in the autumnal hour,
The assailing axe shall come, and sulphurous smoke
Besiege their woody citadel, until
Invading hands usurp their winter store.

Now have the flocks been driven unto the brook,
And bathed to snowy whiteness 'gainst their will;
And, bleating oft beneath the clipping shears,
Have yielded up the fleece. The meadow fields
Are waving in the sunshine like a sea—
A billowy deep, whose flowers are like a foam;
And all abroad, behold the busy throng
Of those who swing the clover, as a path,
From seething scythes into the sidelong swath,
And sharp their blades with many a shrill che-whet.
The air is full of perfume. Following these,
With laugh and song, gay youths, with glittering prongs,
Shake out the scented masses to the sun,
Until the noon beholds the fields half mown,
And from the hill-side calls the midday horn.
Some bands there are, in harvest plains remote,
Who hearken not the conch's announcing call;
But pass into the oak or poplar's shade,

And on the branch suspend the glittering scythes,
Which hang vibrating; then the circle draw—
The grass alike their table and their seat—
While well-stored baskets furnish forth the meal.
The spring near by its crystal tribute gives,
And deals its freshness through the rustic gourd.
When now the grass, oft turned beneath the sun,
Is dry and crisp, and rustles to the tread,
Then comes the rake, with many a long drawn sweep,
Gleaning the shaven weed, until the plain,
Rough with the sultry stacks, appears a field
Thick set with russet tents. And thus it stands
Until the wagons, drawn by horse or yoke
Of easy oxen, with slow swaying gait,
Their large eyes dreaming o'er the rolling cud,
Convey the winter store unto the barn.
Then what wild laughter fills the heated mow,
Where boyhood treads the sweltering waves of hay,
Climbing the encroaching billows as they roll,
Till like a tide it swells along the roof,
Molesting wasps and swallows!—swells and swells,
Till the marauding child, with curious eye,
Thrusts his adventurous hand into the nest—
The highest in the grooved rafters lodged—
And finds but fragments of the tender shell,

Which crumble in his fingers, while outside
The parent bird darts laughing its derision.
  Behold yon shape which, down the dusty road,
Comes marvellously large! It is a form
To frighten childhood from its wayside play;
At whose approach the household mastiff barks,
And, barking, to his kennel shrinks afraid.
It is the pedler, bending 'neath his load,
Like mighty Samson with the Gaza gates,
Or Atlas with the world. His monthly round
Once more hath brought him to these quiet homes.
Once more he lets the monster pack descend,
Straightens his shoulders, and unbinds the straps,
And shows the housewife the enticing store.
Long time she looks, yet shakes the cautious head,
Swaying 'twixt prudence and desire. Meanwhile
The children crowd, with wondering eyes, to see
The motley heap, with fingers oft offending,
And often chid; while, at her apron, one
Clings timidly, and nears, by gradual steps,
As wonder gains the mastery of fear.
With artful words the petty merchant spreads
The various show; now smooths the glossy silk,
And holds it to the light aslant; or, dropped
To lengthened folds, displays the embryo skirt.

There the white lace and there the ribands gleam,
Which light the maiden's eye. The vender's art,
Catching at every favourable sign,
Still pours persuasion from his ready tongue;
And, in the face of many a stubborn "No,"
Lightens his pack and bleeds the matron's purse.

BOOK NINTH.

But this is past, and dies the cloudless day.
How solemnly and calm the evening falls
Around the rural scene! One burning bar
Along the shadowy western hill-top flames,
And, like the blazing iron upon an anvil,
Sinks to a cooler red, and darkly fades,
Leaving the vale to twilight. Charmed hour!
Now fall the dews, of which the blossoms drink
Deep opiate draughts, till, nodding on their stems,
Within their scented mantles folded close,
They dream till morn. The sounds of day are done.
Innumerous tongues, which only wake at eve,
Resume, till night is filled with various notes
Which start the inmost fancy into flight,
Touching the pleasing chords of melancholy,
Until the heart holds sympathy, perforce,

With all the dusk invisible. Above,
The dreary night-hawk wheels on mournful wings,
Like some doomed spirit seeking for its mate,
And pours his bitter wail. Within the deep
Impenetrable sorrow of the woods,
Like one in weeds, with knotted chords of grief
Scourging his heart until it shrieks its wo,
The whip-poor-will lifts up its direful voice.
While, like a demon jeering at their pain,
The owl makes answer with his scornful laugh.
These are sad sounds; and unto Amy's heart —
Although her lover's arm is at her waist,
While their slow feet together brush the path,
Sweeping the shadowy pasture near the grove —
They have a voice prophetic which half drowns
The joy it is her spirit's wont to hear;
And on the wayside grass, methinks, unseen,
One tear-drop more than pensive evening weeps
Is shed. They tell us angels, good and ill,
Attend our steps, to guide or to mislead;
If such be true, with what imploring words,
And clasped hands, and piteous gaze of eyes,
The one oft speaks that would persuade aright,
And in the hour by us securest deemed
Whispers its fears and warns; the while the other

With smiles assuring, safely strews the path
With flowers which lead but to a field of thorns!
If this indeed be true, the instinctive tear,
The shudder, or each inward faint recoil,
Springing we know not whence, should be a voice
To stay the swiftest step—should be a bolt
Transfixing where we stand—a giant rock
Rising, like sudden gates of adamant,
To bar our further course! Alas! too oft,
We lay our hand on the good angel's lip,
And murmur "Peace," whence peace alone can flow;
And list the alluring tongue, whose sweeter words
Pour in the soul the airs which yet shall wake
The prowling storm of discord. "Take this chain"—
So speaks a voice, the while a heated cheek
Flames at her own—"and wear it for my sake."
Then, with a smile, he drops it on her neck;
While in her hand a locket, like an ember,
Glows as the wide moon stares above the east—
Stares, like a ghost, across the maiden's shoulder,
Gazing with Amy on the lover's picture.
Long time she looks, and then, with trembling care,
Within her bosom hides the image dear;
Where on her breast, with wide and stolid eyes,
It lies and warms against her beating heart,

Swaying to each emotion, while the moon
A moment glides behind a fleecy vapour,
And floods it into whiteness like a shroud.
Olivia, with her little taper's light,
Looks from her chamber window to the east—
Looks long with mingled feelings, chiefly hope;
And when a star aslant the zenith drops,
A sigh from out her heart responds, and then
A vision of her gentle friend and lover
Rises; and now amid the Mayday groups,
She once more watches where the reeling dance
Whirls their light forms along, from sun to shade.
So swift is thought that, ere the meteor line
Has faded but a moment from across
The rising constellation in her breast,
The name of Arthur questions every star;
What time each lifts its silvery brow to sight,
And gazes o'er th' horizon's woody bar;—
What news it brings from out the Orient,
What tidings it hath carried in its heart,
Which not the loud pervading sea could drown,
Or time or distance mar? What worbs of love,
What longing westward looks, from those dear lips
And faithful eyes, of one who travels far?
And when the pillow holds her golden hair,

She hears the happiest sounds which charm the night;
But chiefly, from afar, the flashing stream
Which rustles o'er the breastwork at the mill
With ceaseless music. Often—oh, how oft—
By that same sound hath Arthur's ear been soothed
Till slumber weighed with melody his lids!
And sympathizing with the sacred vision
Her fancy sees, the while his name in prayer
Passes, and yet seems lingering on her lips,
A gentle dream before her spirit steals,
Closing the doors of sleep upon her soul.

BOOK TENTH.

What sounds are these which thrill the morning star,
Hailing the advancing banner of the sun,
While now the herald dawn, with backward hair,
Inflates his winding horn, and wakes the day,
Speeding across the hill-tops? Hark, the roll
Of distant cannon rumbling through the sky,
As if a huge triumphal car, in haste,
Were rolling and resounding through the streets
Of some glad city welcoming its return;
While lesser sounds of bells and rattling guns
Swell the rejoicing hour! It is the day
When Independence celebrates her birth—
The Jubilee of Freedom yearly kept!
A nation rising from its rest secure;
A nation which hath never worn a crown;
A land which hath not held a throne, or felt

The foot of king, or seen his purple robe,
Sends up its voice, with one loud shout of joy,
Which starts the eagle of the Nor'most lake,
And wakes the Mexic gulf—while on his shore
The Atlantic hears, and his eternal head
Lifts, and prolongs the sound—till in the West,
On stretching sands, in many an unknown bay,
Mid shadowy slumber the Pacific smiles,
Catching the cadence as it dies, and dreams
Of Freedom's cities rising on his coast,
And navies showing Liberty her flag!
It is a sound to flush the patriot's breast,
And drive the colour from the tyrant's cheek;
Where on his olden and decaying throne,
He stands a-gaze, and, staring o'er the sea,
Wonders; and, with a nervous hand of haste,
Presses the weighty crown upon his brow,
And grasps the sceptre his amaze hath loosed,
Assuring him a king! Long be the day
Remembered, and awaked with shouts, as now!

From every home the gladsome people pour;
O'er woods and fields resound the drum and fife;
And presently the flaming banners, rich
With golden mottoes and with silver stars,
Along the highway set a-blaze the air:

As in the hour when wildly on the sky,
They wrote in words of fire the despot's fall,
Dazzling his dull uncomprehending eye
With "*weighed and wanting!*" till the interpreter,
The father of a grateful country, came
And read the "*Upharsin*" to his startled ear!
With one accord, the various cottage-homes
Pour down the paths and highways to the town—
The village on the white and dusty road—
Their several habitants. The young and old,
Each bent on pleasing and on being pleased,
Are ranged into procession, two by two,
While many a jest and laugh run down the line.
Across the pasture, winding to the grove,
All follow, to the measure of that tune
Which first had birth upon Derision's lips,
Till Victory heard, and with exulting tongue,
Echoed the notes, that, hallowed by her voice,
Henceforth became an anthem for a nation!
Already the rude table's giant length
Stretches beneath the embowering limbs, and scents
The fragrant air with pine. Adjacent, see
The speaker's rostrum—rough, as suits the time,
And strong—where, caught aloft in smooth festoons,
Two silken banners of the stripes and stars,

With friendly points of glittering spear-heads crossed,
Delight the enthusiast's eye. Anon,
Mid shouts, the leaders take the stand; and now
The parson pours the solemn thankful prayer,
The gratitude which every freeman feels.
Then rises Master Ethan, tall and frail,
And clearly, with well modulated voice,
Reads the great "*Declaration*" to the end.
Whereat a long huzza, from every heart,
Shakes the deep welkin, while the limbs between
Murmur afar, and each astonished bird
Drops in the trees and listens. Then arises
The song which every tongue delights to swell.
This past, the fiery speech inflames the hour,
Oft interrupted by the loud applause;
And with a loving ardour lingers long
O'er scenes our grandsires, in the years agone—
What time they held us charmed upon their knees—
Pictured unto our childish eyes, until
The little soul, to patriot's teaching true,
Rose up in arms and waved the mimic sword.
Then comes the plenteous feast, with stated toasts,
And music and gay song between. And now,
In brimming cups the amber cider flows,
Sparkling and sweet, smelling of autumn brown;

Three years a-past from out the creaking press
It streamed, and now full ripe and rich, it glows
In cooling pitchers, starred and striped with dew;
Or paler beverage, where the citron swims,
Yielding the acid from its severed sphere,
And shedding odours of the melting South,
So nectarine, the wasp attracted comes,
An armed republican, and tastes the cup
Ere the libation, at the waiting mouth,
Is pledged to Liberty.

BOOK ELEVENTH.

Thus flies the hour.
Meanwhile, O Muse, withdraw awhile apart,
And note yon figure bending in the woods.
It is the dame of Oakland gathering herbs—
Here plucking liverwort, and there the rank
Hot stems of penny-royal—and, anon,
With crooked fingers, in the easy mould,
Digging the sinuous snake-root, and what else
Her curious knowledge finds. In bundles tied,
These all must at her odorous ceiling hang,
To dry mid swinging sheaves of various mint,
Plucked from the garden and the brook; with sage,
Savouring of Christmas, and wild chamomile,
With bitterer tansy, and the virtuous barks
Of elm and sassafras; with much beside,
Shedding perpetual perfume round the joists,

Forgot, or to the muse unknown. She kneels;
And, as she gathers, mumbles words, unheard,
Whose import none may know except those forms
Invisible which bend the attentive ear,
And catch the faintest breathings of the soul;
Interpreting the murmurs of a child,
The honied accents swarming at its lips,
And the low blended, toothless sounds of age.
Not long she bends when, with a tongue uncouth,
The round Distiller, all a-glow with heat,
Comes fuming like his still; for he hath strode
Throughout the morn across his stretching lands,
Armed with the heavy hickory which he wears,
To note if, in the all-exulting hour,
A foot should dare to trespass on his grounds
Thus, ever, the bad man is seen abroad
Grudging the innocent joy, which others feel,
Impossible to him; while Jealousy,
Within the envious precincts of his heart,
Suggests the wicked act, and, with a smile,
Gloats o'er the cruelty ere it is done.
The fairest landscape may not mould a heart;
A niggard in his palace still is mean;
And cruelty may native be to scenes
Whose loveliness might move another's tears.

See how his set teeth grind in base delight,
And how he strikes from side to side, and beats
A fancied culprit at each blow! He speaks :—
"What bring'st thou, hag, to trespass on these
grounds?
What stealest thou within these woods forbid?"
To which the woman, rising on her staff:—
"I gather simples that thou know'st not of:
Here's this to cool, and here is this which gives
A generous heat when ague numbs the heart.
Oh, I can find all plants, and roots, and barks,
Which Nature's storehouse yields. I know them all;
And, better than your school-diploma'd leech,
Can I prescribe the antidote of ills
Which fire or freeze the blood; but in my art,
I do avow 'fore Heaven, I know no power
Of herb to cool a feverish temper vile,
Or thaw the starving ague of a soul!"
To which the man, with lifted cane, replies:—
"Hence, with a bridle on thy tongue, or else
Beware the weight of this!" When thus the dame,
Shaking her skinny finger o'er her staff:—
"Once came a beggar to a rich man's gate,
Asking the crumbs which from his table fell;
He was refused—perchance thou know'st the rest.

These simples, to the fulness of thy land,
Are less than were the crumbs beneath that table.
All these untended here, self-planted, grow
From year to year, and custom's long consent
Hath yielded them to serve the general use.
I do not trespass, and I do not steal;
Nor shalt thou say it unrebuked. These grounds,
They are not thine save by a legal lie,
Stolen by trick, or bought with devil's blood —
I mean the poison dripping from your still —
And might the wronged man from his coffin rise,
And, with the widow and the orphan, tell
The baseness of thy cunning, the dull ear
Of common justice should be stunned and pained,
And the loud public tongue cry out thy shame,
And retribution, like a bolt of fire
Amid the thunder, fall." E'en as she speaks,
She seems to rise above her wonted height;
Her gray locks falling take the passing breeze,
Her eyes indignant flame, and on her lip
Scorn sits supreme, and mocks the lifted cane.
Meanwhile the blood to the distiller's brow
Mounts with swift madness, and his whole broad face
Burns like a furnace by the bellows blown.
"Hence, witch!" he cries; and reeling from his aim,

With a loud shriek of oaths, he strikes the air,
And striking falls, foaming at mouth, convulsed.
The apoplectic blood, inflamed, hath drowned
His brain; and there, with horrible distort
Of face and frame, he clutching tears the ground.
These are rough touches, but they give the life,
The scars and moles which make the picture true.
And thus he lies until a sauntering group,
Which presently comes by, in wonder stops;
And takes the fallen man in charge, and bears
Him writhing home. The dame, with musing voice,
Speaks as they go, and they may hear who will:—
"Twice hath the mad ox grovelled in the dust,
Dragged by the dogs of anger; when again
They take him to the earth, he shall not rise."
Aud now once more she kneels above her task,
And, digging, traces the eccentric root.

BOOK TWELFTH.

Let us descend afar the summer road,
And note how in the crowded mart is kept
The sacred day. Along the harvest fields,
Throughout the stretching valley, smokes the air
With a long line of the impending dust,
Sultry and thick, until the Sunday garb
Of smoothest black becomes a suit of grey,
And the deep standing grain beside the road
Bows with the collecting weight; while feet
Innumerous are plumping in the dust,
Deep as the fetlocks, as it were a snow;
And flying wheels fling from their tires and spokes
Invisible the choking cloud. Behold the inn,
Midway between the village and the town,
Where waves the starry flag across the way,
Swung from the house-top to the opposing tree,

A silken arch of triumph. O'er the porch
Swarm out and in, like bees about a hive,
The noisy people whom the keeper greets
With smile incessant and unfailing joke.
Lo, how the hot air reeks with the perfume
Of crushing mint, in potent glasses drowned,
And smoke of Cuban weed; or, stronger yet,
Of rank plant cultured in Kentuckian fields.
From either side the high and pendulous sign
The painted eagle looks, with spreading wings,
As if to sentinel the coming guest.
But 'neath his shade, with an unchecking rein,
Behold yon party pass! Olivia there,
Between her parents, sits with glowing cheeks.
Thus ride they on until, beyond the hill,
In the far smoky landscape, winding slow,
They catch with eager gaze the silvery line
Of tranquil Delaware; so distance-veiled,
The eye, unaided, scarcely notes the sail
Brooding in middle of receding plains.
Then bursts the glowing city on the view;
Waking a pleasurable sense which none
So deep in soul can feel as they who bring
The mind well stored with rural love, and wear
At heart the freshness of the summer fields.

Thus, in lost ages of the long ago,
The rustic swains, girded with simple skins,
From Carmel's side or cedared Lebanon,
Beheld the gorgeous city at their feet;
What time the yearly festival enticed,
Its thousand banners swelling on the wind,
And every breeze with music jubilant,
And gates all wide. Or thus the pilgrim band,
Aweary with long travel, sore of feet,
Turning some point of the Abruzzian mount,
Beholds the plain, and Tiber winding dim,
And the long stretch of ancient aqueducts,
Striding like caravans the blue champaign;
Till, lo! the Roman capitol appears,
Crowned with the dome which crowns the world!
Anon, the Schuylkill, sacred to the barge of mirth,
Its green banks consecrate to pleasure's paths,
Winds into sight with many a silvery curve;
And at the breast-work, with a ceaseless voice,
Rustles the music which its waters learned,
On mountain wilds remote, where Carbon's hills
Hear in their inmost heart the miner's stroke.
Behold the mound by art and nature reared,
"Fairmount!" in whose tall top the waters lie
Lifted as in a great baptismal font;

The height from whence the river deity
Pours, from his giant and refreshing urn,
The stream which slakes a grateful city's thirst.
But fancy this; for yet no statue there,
Worthy the place, above his liquid task
Stands to the four winds, beautiful and bright,
Gazing upon the city which he laves,
While the glad city gazes back to him.
Oh! wherefore rises not the marble pile
Above this green and consecrated height?
Not one, but many, one above the rest,
Looking like Allegheny o'er his hills.
Lo, how it bathes unnumbered miles of streets—
A great heart pulsing through far crystal veins—
Where, but a few short generations since,
The Indian stretched his lazy sombre length;
And the red deer stooped, undeterred, and drank,
Or, 'neath the chestnut or the walnut shade,
Cropped the rank grass at leisure. At the Bridge,
The horses sudden tramp the sounding planks;
Where passes oft the Connestoga team,
Ringing its own announcement of approach,
With shoulder-shaken bells—a monster wain,
Slow, rumbling, and which oft in winter sends
The shrilly creak from frosty wheels afar.

How the white noon awakes to the report
Of all explosive engines known to man,
From the sharp cracker to the roaring bass
Of cannon, answering from square to square!
At every proclamation shaking earth,
And rattling every window; while the scent
Of wasted powder loads each breath inhaled,
As in some town resisting when besieged.
From street to street the party takes its way,
Gazing on the processions as they pass
With wondering admiration. There they see,
In costly uniform, the shining troops
Of armed volunteers; or there the long,
Proud lines of labour, honouring their trades,
Parading with bright banners; and the stout,
Brave firemen decked in helmet and in cape —
A conflagration pictured upon each —
Their costly engine wreathed about with flowers —
Drawing as 'twere a conqueror's car. No day,
Of all the year, is so alive as this;
No other day hath this calm city been
So driven from staid propriety, and waked
To such wild, joyous riot; save that time
When youthful feet ran boundless through the streets,
To fix the childish gaze on one who came

Welcomed with honour's highest, last excess—
The honour only rivaled by the love—
Taking his glorious way with roses strewn,
And under endless bannered arches, starred
With one proud name, still sacred—"La Fayette!"
    And still the party wander down the street,
Oft gazing on the snowy marble pile;
Or stroll into the crowded squares, and walk
Beneath the shade of ancient forest trees,
Greeting them as all friends. Oh, wherefore, ye
Who hold the welfare of the town at heart,
And wield its destinies, will ye behold
The city, with its hot and rapid heat,
Trample the woods and blight the fields; nor leave
One ampler space where, on a day like this,
The thankful throng may walk abroad, and feel
The pleasure which it is to breathe the air
Which, unimpeded by the heated walls,
Takes health and freshness from the leaves it stirs,
And gives to whom inhales? Nor yet too late,
While those wide spaces—full of sun and shade,
And antique trees, with daily trembling filled
And apprehension of the approaching axe—
O'er Schuylkill spread their asking arms, and call
Aloud for your protection. Ere the street,

With frequent ringing of the builder's trowel,
Usurps their quiet depth, go boldly forth;
And, with your powerful wand of office, draw
The boundary line which none shall dare invade.
And every tree, thus rescued, when the crowds
Of future generations walk beneath,
Shall whisper to their grateful ears your name;
And be a vernal monument, each year,
Renewing honour to the rescuer.

BOOK THIRTEENTH.

Here, stranger, stay! This is the sacred spot
Which knew the patriots in the years agone.
Here trod the noblest form the land has known;
Here swelled the stoutest soul e'er form has held;
And here—nor here alone, but round the world,
And throughout heaven—my faith will have it so—
The name most loved is spoken, and rolls on
Revered by freemen, and by angels breathed,
And trembling oft upon the lips of slaves,
Brightening their dream of hope. Still to our hearts
Let the great name of Washington be dear;
And faithful as the star is to the night,
Or as Niagara to his cataract true,
Let the increasing stream of praise be poured
From off a nation's tongue. This is the spot:
Here is the hallowed hall where bravely met

Freedom's stout conclave, pledging lives and honour;
And this the terrace, looking to the square,
Where Liberty's apostles, all a-glow
With the wild ardour of the hour, came forth,
And, to the applauding patriot crowd without,
Read the great chart ere yet the names were dry.
This is the place: and there, upon the step,
Behold, where sits yon figure scarred and grey,
His stout staff taking palsy from his hand,
And shaking on the door-stone. Here, once more,
He pays the yearly visit to the spot,
And lives in memory all the glorious past;
And thus unto the group of listeners gives
The visions of gone days, as one by one
They rise before his spiritual eye.

"Lo, now the cannon thundering to the sky,
The thickening fumes that scent the heated air,
Recall the camp, and spread before mine eye
The pitch of battle and the triumph there.

The summoned ploughman grasps the ready gun,
And swiftly strides across the furrow's sod;
The smith, ere half the heated shoe is done,
Swings on in haste, and rides the steed unshod.

The mason flings his glittering trowel by,
  And leaves behind the pale and weeping few;
The miller's wheel above the stream hangs dry,
  While o'er the hill he waves the swift adieu.

Lo, all the air is throbbing to the drum;
  In every highway sounds the shrilly fife;
And flashing guns proclaim afar they come,
  Where hurried banners lead the way to strife.

Though rude the music, and the arms are rude,
  And rustic garments fill the motley line,
Yet noble hearts, with noble hopes imbued,
  Thrill through the ranks with energy divine.—

Thrill through the ranks until those sounds become
  Celestial melodies from Freedom's lips!
These arms an engine to strike despots dumb,
  And leave oppression howling in eclipse.

Then comes the struggle, raging loud and long—
  The seven years' battle with the banded foes—
The tyrant, and the savage, and the strong
  Grim arm of want with all its direful woes.

Half clad and barefoot, bleeding where they tread,
Where hunger and disease allied consort,
The pale survivors stand among their dead,
And brave the winter in their snow-walled fort.

But heavier than the storms which fold the Earth,
Than all the ills which winter's hand commits,
The bitter thought that at the sacred hearth
Of unprotected homes some horror sits.

But God is just; and they who suffer most,
Win most; for tardy triumph comes at last!
The patriot, bravely dying at his post,
Hath rivalled all the Cæsars of the past.

Right conquers wrong, and glory follows pain,
The cause of Freedom vindicated stands;
And heaven consents; while, staring o'er the main,
Old Europe greets us with approving hands.

If now a film o'er-swim my aged gaze,
Or if a tremour in my voice appear,
It is the memory of those glorious days
Which moves my failing frame and starts the tear.

Oh, on this sacred spot again to rest,
  Where passed the patriots, ere this old heart faints!
Then I depart, with a contented breast,
  Where they are walking crowned among the saints.

Here on these steps, made holy by their tread,
  I list their kindling voices as of yore;
And hear that bell, now hanging speechless, dead,
  Which rung for Freedom, broke, and rung no more.

Broke with the welcome tidings on its tongue,
  Broke, like a heart, with joy's excessive note
'Tis well no cause less glorious e'er hath rung
  In silver music from its hallowed throat."

BOOK FOURTEENTH.

BEHOLD the river, wide, respiring, vast,
Swelling and falling, answering to the main.
Here rise and sink the multitudinous ships,
Swaying in slumberous ease, where every flag
Known to a Christian sky salutes the air.
How the brown cordage like a net-work spreads,
A monster web entangling leafless pines!
From this same wharf, down dropping with the tide,
Went Arthur, when he bade his last adieu—
While the great bay, as usherer to the sea,
Unto the ocean's awful presence led—
Where stands the maid in secret musing held,
While from the charmed fountains of her soul
The longing tear upwells. The sun descends;
And like a startling meteor in the sky,
The whizzing rocket streaks the twilight air,

And curving up the azure deep afar,
Explodes with muffled sound, and lights the eve
With momentary stars of various hue.
In swift succession how they soar and burst,
Answered from all the quarters of the town,
Till oft the sky is full of falling lights;
As on that memorable autumn night,
When rained the heavens a thick meteoric shower,
Puzzling the wise astronomers at watch,
And shaking many a sturdy soul with fear,
Till superstition, with affrighted voice,
Proclaimed the day of doom. From yon green isle,
Which like a war-ship on the water lies,
The arrowy signals chiefly fly; while come
The joyous habitants and crowd the wharves,
The ships, the ferries, barges and batteaux,
And skiffs that glide between, while every house
From base to roof o'erflows. And now the night,
While every face unto the island looks,
Falls deeply down; and all the curious stars
People the dark and crowding, group o'er group,
Gaze from the shadowy terraces of heaven,
And wonder at the fires that mock their light.
Hark, the loud rattle, like artillery!
And note the phantom lustre on each face,

Swift changing through the iris scale of hues,
Most strange and beautiful, thrown from yon wheel
Which from its flails of fire flings the light sparks
Like chaff upon the air, with whinings loud,
While admiration flies from face to face.
Nor this alone; wheel after wheel is fired,
Whirling continuous, discharging lights
Innumerous as summer's dust; until
Behold the flaming chariot appears,
A swift triumphal car ablaze with gems,
And flying through a crowd of welcoming roses,
Where Liberty a starry goddess rides,
While o'er her head her favourite eagle sails
On guardian wings of fire. And suddenly
A temple lifts its constellated front,
Swinging its great arch, drawn in blazing lines,
Athwart the dark with architecture strange,
Inspiring, grand; as if the stars of heaven
Should sweep together, clustering into form,
To show the world the dome where freedom dwells.
And lo! the glorious vision in the tide
Inverted hangs in wavering lines of light:
Such is the pyrotechnist's art. And now
The sky vibrates with the prolonged applause;
The lights die out; the night resumes its sway,

While peace and silence close the festive gates.
    Olivia, weary, to her pillow strange
Resigns her cheek, while through her wakeful brain
The visions of the day, in clear review,
Pass one by one, and fright the wings of sleep.
Hour after hour, the watchman's sounding tread
And solemn voice alarm the sinking lid,
And wake the thought afresh; till, presently,
The whirling rattle and the startling cry
Of "fire!" too frequent heard, disturb the town,
Breaking the charm of midnight; while reply,
From spire and tower, the wild and direful bells,
Directing with their strokes the engines' course,
Which now fly thundering to assail the blaze,
And soon to conquer. Rising on the sky,
Destruction's banner, like a boreal light,
Dilates and brightens till the maiden's room,
Though safe, is full of splendour like a noon.
She hears the frequent heavy brakes descend,
Mingled with voices and with hurrying feet,
Till gradually the drowned flame submits,
While slowly dies the hue from out her chamber.
And now once more the quiet, like a bird
Untimely startled from its nest, refolds
Its wings, and drops through visions into sleep.

BOOK FIFTEENTH.

WHEN I recount the pleasant sights of earth—
Fair childhood blowing bubbles in the sun—
A pleasure party, in a moonlit barque;
The little sail with breeze and music swelled—
A dancing wreath of children crowning May—
A bridal group across a distant field
Returning, with gay footsteps, from the church—
I can recall no brighter, nobler scene,
Than men at labour mid the waving grain,
When summer, with its alchemy, transmutes
The crops from green to gold! The harvest sun
Burns broad and white above the yellowing world,
Which, for its plenty, laughs a rustling laugh;
A voice which cheers the hearts of those who strode
Athwart the yielding ground, with swinging hands,
In springtime, casting bread upon the earth,

To be returned a hundred fold. The air
Hangs hot and silent, save where yonder bird,
The meadow-lark, darts into sudden voice
From out the grain, and in the next tree lights,
And, panting, sings no more; or where, perchance,
The Oriole, careless of its swinging nest,
From whence the young have flown, a moment streaks
The sky with fire and song, and then gives o'er;
Or yon tricoloured bird, with nervous haste
Ascending spirally the sapless trunk,
Drums loudly as he climbs; or locust hid
Swift springs his shrilly rattle; or the small
Green insect, greener than the grass it bends,
With the field cricket lifts its jarring voice;
While his grey brother, on ambitious wings,
Flickers his short flight down the summer road,
Oft dropping in the sultry sand. Behold
The yellow, dainty-pinioned swarm arise,
On simultaneous wings, as soars a flame;
Or, settling where the small spring blots the dust,
Glow like a golden group of butter-cups.

What a calm realm of sunshine gleams the world!
The aspen only feels a phantom breath;
Beneath the great tree's shadow in the field
The silent cattle stand; and in the cool

Deep shade of garden shrubs the fowls are hid,
Fluttering the dust upon their wings, with eye
Suspicious watching oft the hawk which sails,
Noiseless as sleep, upon the lofty air.
Beside the spring, where the tall sycamore,
And one wide willow, roof the cooling spot,
The dairy maid is singing mid her pans,
And skimming off the deep and yellow cream,
While floats abroad the sweet delicious scent
Of cedar from the scalded churn. And now,
With many a rumbling splash, the dasher flies,
Forcing the cream which oozes at the lid.
At length the gathering weight, which lifts and falls,
Denotes the labour through. In days like these,
An hour suffices to transmute the mass,
Which oft, in winter, whirls from morn till noon,
Or later still, refusing to obey—
Withheld, as some have deemed, by witch's charm.
Along the wayside fence, by briery roads,
The ruddy children, with their fingers stained,
Collect the berries which, with milk combined,
Shall to the reaper's hearty palate give
The luscious dessert when the meat is past.
The full fields, like a shepherd's flock in spring,
Yield up their fleeces, till the well-bound sheaves,

In glowing stacks, nod o'er the stubbled farm.
Now sounds the horn 'neath the meridian sun;
And the brown labourers, hurrying to the call,
Beside the deep well lave their heated brows;
Where oft the bucket from the windlass drops,
Rattling till deluged, then, ascending slow,
Comes dripping to the brink, and sends abroad
A cool and grateful freshness. Then behold
Where sweeps the table wide, from door to door,
Looking from east to west. With open brow
The generous matron welcomes in the group;
And there Olivia, not too proud to tend,
But with a flush of pleasure on her face,
Glides gracefully from chair to chair, and helps
The glowing reaper's plate; here fills the glass
With odorous cider, sparkling as it flows,
Or draws the bowl with liquid from the churn,
Cooled at the spring beside the yellow prints.
Here smokes the ample joint, and steaming there
The yellow ears of maize inviting stand,
Fresh from the cauldron drained—delicious food,
To other lands unknown—with much beside.
When this is past, the berries crown the board,
The whortle from the wood, and those at morn
Plucked from the wayside briers. The garden, too,

And orchard lend their fulness to the hour;
For 'tis the season when the generous year
Pours from his plenteous horn the ripened fruit—
The mellow peach, and bursting purple plum,
The early apple, and the golden pear;
But chiefly the huge melon which, when ripe,
Yields, to the pressing hands and listening ear,
A crisp and frosty sound, from out its heart
Of crimson snow, that calls the thirsty knife.
Thus flies the noon, until the heated fields
Recall to labour, and the day goes by.
Now, when the eve sets in, and one by one
The stars come leaping o'er the eastern bar,
And the great moon, aflush with summer heat,
Climbs lazily along the harvest sky—
Where dart the fire-flies with eccentric course,
Oping their frequent dainty lantern-doors,
As if to find a treasure lost—the group
Of reapers gather on the social porch,
And pass the shadowy hour in language meet
The season and the place. And much they talk
Of news which lately, from the far off West,[3]
Startled the calm community; as when
Some foreign sound disturbs the labouring hive—
Or bee, returning from exploring search,

Proclaims a land of more enticing sweets,
And wakes a general buzz throughout the swarm.
The younger men are restless to be gone,
And descant largely on the wild pursuit
Of game, exhaustless in the boundless woods.
Some shake the doubtful head—the older these—
And tell of labours long to be endured—
The battle with the forest, and the stern
Privation to be borne, where oft the call.
Of chill necessity affrights the soul;
Repeating tales their childhood frequent heard
From sires who mid these hills and valley came,
And, with the guardian fire-arm at their side,
Laid the loud axe unto the woodland foot.
But what was meant to caution and deter,
Inflames the youthful fancy and desire;
And even age detects along his veins
A curious yet an unacknowledged glow,
And feels an impulse rising in his breast
He hath not felt for years; and, to conceal
How much his spirit echoes younger thought,
Puts by the subject with some careless jest,
And turns the converse on to-morrow's task.
Now see where strides, o'er many a homeward field,
The hired labourer to his lowly cot:

The shouldered sickle, by the moonshine lit,
Gleams like a rising crescent. At the door
His happy wife, and happier children, stand
And welcome his return. Then to his couch,
To others hard, luxurious to him,
Softened by toil, he turns and drains the cup—
The drowning cup of sleep—unto the dregs.

BOOK SIXTEENTH.

On yonder hill, with oak and hickory crowned,
What sight is that which draws, from far and near,
The thronging people up the dusty roads,
And through each field where'er a by-path leads?
See, where the red and new-arisen sun
Points his bright finger through the upland grove,
Flushing the white tents to a rosy hue!
And hark, the call of the resounding horn,
Which echo, from yon hill, with slumberous shell
Blows softly back! Are these the tents of war,
By some proud general pitched, where bayonets gleam,
And sentinels walk, and banners to the drum
Dance in mid air, and flap their sanguine folds?
It is the camp of that increasing strife
Waged 'gainst a world of sin; it is a host
Come out upon the glorious side of Truth,

To fight, to suffer, and, with love, to conquer!
With songs triumphal under flags of peace,
Spread like the wings of swans upon the wind,
They hold their siege against the walls of Wrong,
And will not rest till on the highest tower
Which crowns his ramparts that white banner floats.
There Wesley's spirit hovers, and, with voice
Clear as a bugle winding, mid the hills,
The soul of Whitfield soars. There, with long beard
Sweeping his patriarchal breast, arrives
The apostle-pilgrim, punctual to the hour—
Lorenzo, the eccentric—and at once
Mounts the rough desk, and lifts his startling voice,
While eager thousands crowd the space to look;
And seeing, hear; and every neighbouring tree
Is populous with faces forward bent.
Here, scoffer, smooth the scorn from off thy lip;
Nor you, nor I, though holding faith divine,
May sit in judgment and condemn the scene.
Though we approve not, wiser heads than ours
Have bowed and worshipped at the woodland altar,
And pressed the temporary couch at night
Within the wavy tent, and often found
The peace which they had sought elsewhere in vain.
Let us not waste the vigour of our minds

In acrimonious quarrel over creeds.
Not ours the business of dispute; but ours,
Ye gentle hearts for whom I chiefly sing,
The pleasing duty to find good in all;
And, finding, recognize and own in each
A brotherhood, no difference of faith
May set afar. Nor Brahmin, Turk, nor Jew,
Nor he who kneels to Deity in stones—
The savage instinct searching for its God—
Each seeking truth the nearest way he knows,
Shall wake in me one cold condemning word—
While Charity, the sweetest child of Heaven,
Hides her bright face, and weeps behind her wings—
But love instead. And we will interchange
Whatever thought may cheer each other on;
For all are pilgrims on one darksome road:
One may have store of water and no bread;
The other bread, and faint with sultry thirst;
One plenteous oil, another but dry wick.
Hence is our duty plain; and simple need,
Left to itself, would teach us oft aright;
While prejudice, by doctrines of a sect,
Would leave us hungry, thirsty, or at night
Give but a lightless lantern. Let who will
Quarrel o'er outward forms: so quarrelled they

Who gambled for the garments of our Lord,
And heard not the deep agony of soul
Of Him who cast all mantles by as vain,
And died for simple truth.

BOOK SEVENTEENTH.

THE summer flies,
And autumn slowly comes, his withering breath
Crisping whate'er he breathes on; and the woods
He sets ablaze with gorgeous hues which burn,
With noiseless flame, until the foliage falls,
Strewing the ground like embers, while the limbs
Spread to the sky their empty ashen arms.
At her lone window, drawn from household cares
Olivia sits, and to her lover writes;
And thus the ardour of her fancy flows:
"The months go by, the seasons slow depart,
With steps reluctant, looking to the time
When thou wert here—how different their flight!
I think one half the sunshine went with thee,
And, like my thoughts, the better half. And now,
The dreary autumn comes, the sighing days,

With which my heart seems strangely set in tune.
Here, where I gaze, I see the stubbled fields,
The reddening forest, and the misty air—
All sights and sounds which make the soul alone.
Day after day, the flying flocks go south,
In living lines, which write along the sky
The prophecy of winter's sure approach;
I hear at night their voices o'er the roof,
Mingled with whirring wings. On yonder plain
The rustling maize, in many a bowing shock,
Whispers to every passing breeze. Last night,
Beneath the white moon, in the silent air,
In jovial bands the huskers, flocking, came,
And stripped the covers from the yellow ears,
And left them glowing there in golden mounds.
Oh, how the song, and jest, and laugh, went round!
And when the crimson ear was found, the prize
Was held in blazing splendour, like a torch,
And all proclaimed a 'sweetheart,' and rejoiced.
I stood apart, and, as in days a-gone,
Hearkened to hear thy voice among the rest;
But there were none so happy or so clear,
Or, as I fancied, half so musical.
Within doors, through the busy afternoon,
Till late at eve, the neighbouring dames and maids

Found social pleasure round the spreading quilt,
With rapid hands, till on the oft-rolled frame
The latest puffy diamond-row was stitched.
Then, when the gay and separate tasks were done,
And noisy supper past, the room was cleared;
When mirth, and music, and the mazy dance
Reeled through the night till every rafter rang,
And the wide floor, beneath the gliding feet,
Swayed till each long joist, half-astonished, groaned.
I could not dance, and could not join the glee;
Each smile I forced was half akin to tears;
So clearly came the old times o'er my mind.
To-day the orchard yields its glowing fruits,
Which tumble, widely, with a thunderous sound,
Shaken from stormy limbs—a monster hail.
And there the creaking cider-press is fed,
And oozes the sweet liquid through the straw,
Where gather the inebriate bees and wasps;
And childhood imitates the winged thieves
With wheaten pipes which yield the nectar draught.
The sweetened air across the casement floats,
And merriment invites abroad. Ah, me!
How pining Memory flies into the past,
And lives in the departed scene—so fond,
She cannot taste the pleasure of to-day!

Then were we children, and in hours like this
None were more happy. It is now the time
When slumber seems to hover on the air.
O'er all the veil of Indian summer floats,
Blue, thin, and silent, lovely as a dream—
A dream which, presently, the North shall wake,
The shrewish North, with shrilly tongue of storm
The sounding flails, and Bowman's beating loom,
Pulse through the brooding air. From out yon barn
Floats the loud tempest of the sweeping fan;
While, on the stormy gust its wings create,
Beyond the door the winnowed chaff is blown
Swarming like golden bees. E'en where I sit,
I can behold the great wheel of the mill
Flashing its silvery circles in the sun,
And yet so distant cannot hear its song.
All happiest sights and sounds seem held afar.
In the dear light of memory thou dost stand;
I see thee smile yet cannot hear thy voice.
It is the season when the woodland trees,
Through yellow fingers, shed the plenteous nuts;
When happy children, from the school released,
Wander from grove to grove. Canst thou not yet
Bring back to fancy those departed days
When we, together, with our baskets went,

Shelling the walnuts till our little hands
Were like the autumn's brown? or chestnuts found
Dropped from their starry burrs? or with the squirrels,
Beneath the hickory, shared the shellbark's store?
How then we spread them in the loft to dry,
Between the rolls of wool for winter wheels—
The loft made odorous by the bundled herbs?
Ah, yes, thou needs must often see it all,
And, seeing, sigh for the delightful hours.
Oft have I prayed for thy return—how oft!—
But chiefly now, for these are changeful times.
Loud Rumour's voice entices to the West—
The call from out the backwoods daily comes—
The only topic when the neighbours meet;
And the excitement like a fever spreads,
Contagious, till one cannot safely say
Who, ere another summer, may depart
To be immured in the far forest's gloom.
The drover, with his cattle passing by,
Tells marvellous stories of that plenteous land,
Inflaming all he meets. And frequently
A letter from its three weeks journey rests,
Breathing of woods primeval, and confirms
The floating tale, advising all to come.
Even round our fireside spreads the exciting theme.

Wert thou but here, to join in the exploit,
The wilderness were welcome as the town."
And more she writes; but let the veil be drawn
Between the world and her more tender thoughts.

BOOK EIGHTEENTH.

Now comes the master's jovial, motley day,
Remnant of troublous times; and after this
Election follows. To the neighbouring town
The farmers flock, and gathering in crowds,
Discuss their candidates with growing warmth;
Then drop the powerful scrip into the poll—
The little weight which turns a nation's scale—
Where oft a world-wide interest is weighed
Beyond recall, and settled. Let no vote
Be dropped with careless thought; for it may be
The last strong hand which draws the lever down
Which moves the giant destiny of man.

No future shall replace what power is yours,
Ye heirs of what the patriots bequeathed.
The hand which holds a plough is strong as that,
And stronger oft, than which a sceptre grasps.

Then be ye each as watchful as a king,
And jealous of your rights; yet generous,
As only freemen can afford to be.
Behold where walks the white-haired beldame, Frost,
Breathing her bitterness o'er all the scene —
She whom erewhile we hailed as maiden Dew.
The flowers she fed, when morning-glories blew
Their white and purple trumpets to the dawn,
Are nipped and withered by her fingers cold;
The grass is crisp and brittle 'neath her tread;
And, like a witch, she flies the broad clear sun,
But works her charm beneath the gibbous moon
See, where the joyous hallow-eve comes in,
And how the country is awaked to mirth!
While, far and near, the sleepless watch-dog's bark
Responds from farm to farm, till oft the wife
Starts from her couch to peer with anxious eye;
Or, on her troubled pillow, dreams of harm
In cabbage plots or poultry sheds sustained.
Round many a hearth, in noisy groups, collect
The youths and maids, and there Pomona reigns.
Swift flies the apple to the paring blade,
While, like a serpent, falls the coiling peel.
Some quarter and take out the core, and some
Attend the giant cauldron o'er the fire,

Which on the huge crane stretched from jamb to jamb,
Wide as a gate that lets a chariot pass,
Swings o'er the blaze with cider steaming hot,
Where the brown stirrer with its handle long
A ceaseless motion keeps. Thus flies the night,
Until the odorous mass grows thick and dark,
Which then is dipped in various jars to cool.
And now the reel, to some rude Afric's viol,
Whirls through the shadowy hour till oft the star
Of morning lights the laughing revellers home.
Lo, now the ungentle time of slaughter comes,
And horrid preparation frights the hour.
The flashing knives upon the grinding disk
Are held, with grating and discordant noise;
And the great casks with scalding water smoke,
Where oft the red-hot stone falls hissing, drowned.
The muse, affrighted, flies the barbarous scene,
And seeks, elsewhere, whatever rural sights
Engage the autumn day. Beside the barn,
Some break the brittle flax with swingle loud,
And on the thorny hackle cleanse from tow.
Some, where the full cribs like a sunset gleam,
Shedding a golden lustre, shell the ears
Of Indian corn preparing for the mill;
Or thresh the buckwheat which on many a morn,
When Boreas on the frosty panes shall breathe,

Fresh from the griddle shall delight the board.
And there the matron by her cottage door,
With numerous wicks on slender twigs arranged,
In melting cauldrons gives the fragrant dip,
Preparing tapers for the winter's eve;
Which then, suspended in the air to cool,
Hang like the icicles at frozen roofs,
That harden as the sinking sun departs.

Now through the heavens the changing vapours fly,
Driven by winds eccentric, threatening storm,
While answering shadows sweep the stubbled land.
Together smite the woodland's empty arms,
While, with the last leaves, fall the latest nuts.
Along the ground the rustling foliage whirls,
Where oft the quail from out the sickled fields,
Affrighted, comes, in kindred coloured drifts,
To seek a rescue from the hunter's eye.
And there the squirrel, with his pattering feet,
Collects his winter store; or on a limb,
The highest 'gainst the sky, with blowing bush,
Sits swinging o'er the leafless world amazed.
At length the slanting, chill November rain
Usurps the landscape wide, and with its hand—
Agued and blue with penetrating cold—
Closes the slumberous barn, and every door,
Most hospitable, shuts.

BOOK NINETEENTH.

THE winter comes,
Proclaimed by winds, and charioted by snows;
And, like an arctic voyager returned,
His white furs breathing of the Nor'land frost,
Tells of the frozen fields and mounts of ice,
For ever flaming in the boreal lights,
A-flush with dawn-like hues which bring no day.
Now the bright sun above a brighter world—
A world as white as last month's perfect moon—
Looks all abroad, and on the jewelled trees,
And icicles which taper at the eaves,
Flashes his lavish splendour. Every stream
Is deeply sealed beneath a frozen bridge,
Where glides the glittering skate, with many a whirl,
Scarring the polished floor. Afar and near
The air is full of merriment aud bells;

And the swift sleigh, along the slippery road,
Flies through the powdery mist which every gust
Blows from the buried field. Here sweep some past,
Muffled in generous skins — the bison's robe
Spread largely, trailing in the sidelong drift.
There timid Amy by her lover sits,
Her soft cheek blushing at the winter's kiss.
Anon, behold the temporary sledge —
Built in the first joy of the earliest snow —
Which gives to rustic youths a thrill of pleasure
Deeper than feels the Czar, encased in furs,
Mid music swifter and more safely whirled.
Down yonder hill, mid boyhood's ringing shouts,
An avalanche of little sleds are shot,
Streaking the air with laughter as they fly.
There the tough snow-balls, hardened 'twixt the knees,
Stream through the air, with meteor-crossing lines,
Till oft the winter coat is starred with white,
The mark of skilful aim. Here one, perchance,
Starts the small round, which gathers as it rolls,
Until the giant pile half blocks the road;
Or at the wayside reared, takes human form —
A monster bulk that, when the eve sets in,
Shall fright the traveller with its ghostly shape,
And start his steed aside. In yonder shed,

Where rings the anvil with a bell-like sound,
The Smith, while oft the share is in the coals,
Leans on the polished handle of his sledge,
And sees in visions, pleasing to his eye,
The pictures which the floating rumours give
Enticing to the West. And when the iron
Flames on the stithy, like a rising sun,
Driving the shadows into cobweb corners,
The hammer takes new impulse from his arm—
Imagination so possesses him—
And falls as 'twere the echo-waking axe,
Swung by a pioneer in boundless woods.
The Wheelwright, too, wields the curved, dangerous
adze,
And shapes the axle, as it were a beam
Or rafter for the cabin, in his mind.
The Mason—for the frozen mortar now
Refuses use—beside the glowing fire,
Spreads his hard hands, and, gazing in the blaze,
Startles the woodlands with his trowel's ring.
The Cooper, at his shaving-horse astride,
Draws the swift knife, and shapes the oaken stave
As 'twere a shingle for his forest home.
The Miller hears, amid the dusty meal,
The mill-dam roaring at some unknown stream,

And rears his pulpit in the distant wild.
And in the grove the Woodman, mid his cords,
Fells the primeval trunks. And e'en the Gunner—
So powerful the infectious fever grows—
Strides, heedless of the rising flocks of quail;
And, homeward turning, hangs the weapon up,
Saving his charge for more important game.
Now comes the warmer noon. The vanes swing round
Before the south wind's soft and venturous wing.
The breeze, like childhood in the shell-bark limbs,
Shakes from the trees the rattling sleet; and now
The eaves are pouring as with summer rain.
Along the slushy roads the labouring sleigh,
Returning, cuts into the softened earth,
Grating discordant to the bells; the driver's face,
Each melting moment falling with the thaw,
Gives the long gauge of disappointed mirth.
Then follows eve. The slanting sun descends—
The snow grows crisp—the roofs withhold their rain—
And, like a proud man's mind, the icicle,
Which had been spendthrift once, gives less and less,
Until the last slow drop is held congealed,
And the cold, miser point forbids approach.

When o'er the western threshold goes the sun,
Spreading his great hand through the crimson clouds,

Shedding his benediction ere he leaves,
Then dawns the eve around the social fire;
From six to ten the nightly quiet glows,
Soothing the household. Oh, how blest are they
Who feel the calm that gilds the sacred hearth!
To them, nor spring, nor summer's voiceful time,
Hold music sweeter than is chaunted there.
From out the steaming logs the woodland sprites
Sing, as they fly, a grateful song of peace;
And crickets, full of harvest memories,
In nook and crevice warm, rehearse their lays,
Until the charmed and dreamy sense beholds
The scented hay-fields, and the nodding sheaves;
While Winter, like an uninvited guest,
Stands at the hearth forgot. What though the morn,
Through darkened chambers, pours her phantom snow,
While all the stars, which ice the arch of heaven,
Pierce the deep stillness with their splintered light;—
Or though the clouds their fleecy fulness shed,
Till farm with farm become one fenceless field,
And fill the road, and roof the running brook,
To oft mislead the wagoner and his team;—
Though 'gainst the cottage piles the shifting snow,
While at the sill the searching powder sifts;—

Far from the blaze the deepening cold withdraws,
And all grow tranquil as the tempest swells.
    Thus flames the hearth where Master Ethan sits,
In dreamy trance, who, gazing at the blaze,
Beholds Elijah's mounting wheels of fire;
While, at his feet, the glowing grandchild, rapt,
Pours o'er some magic page; or, eager lists,
With largening eyes, the reverend tongue discourse
Of troublous days when War bestrode the land.
On her low chair the dozing grandam knits,
The needles moving when her eyes are closed,
Till the dropped stitch requires the ready aid
Of younger sight and hands. Still at her wheel
Olivia dreams with misty, brooding eye,
While flies the flax between her fingers warm,
And on the spindle grows the oval spool.
And there the larger wheel, whose whirring loud
Makes through the house a tempest of its own,
The matron drives; and, pacing forth and back,
Smooths the white rolls that dwindle as they go.
The easy farmer o'er the journal pours;
Or, musing, clears the western forest lands,
And sows his harvest in the ashen field;
Or drives his plough into the deep, rank soil
Of boundless prairies stretching to the sky,

Till fancy fills the crescent of his hope.
No chilling sound disturbs the pleasing dream;
In vain the winds besiege his stable-walls
Where, mid the well-filled racks, his cattle lie.
And now, responsive to the village spire,
The cock proclaims the hour, and all is well;
While shadowy Time, who stands upon the stair,
Lifts his clear voice, and points his warning hand.
Anon, the flames in ashen depths expire,
And none but crickets cheer the cooling hearth.
Peace bars the doors, Content puts out the lamp,
And Sleep fills up the residue of night.
And still, as sounds the hour-announcing spire,
The crowing cock makes answer, "all is well!"

BOOK TWENTIETH.

APPROACHES now the time to Christians dear,
Hallowed with grateful memories; the hour
Which startled Herod on his throne, and drew
The star-led Magi through the manger door,
Where lay the infant Saviour of a world,
More terrible to Eden's serpent vile—
Which now, affrighted, backward shrunk, chagrined,
Coiling upon himself—than was the boy,
The cradled Hercules, unto the snake
He strangled in his grasp. This is the eve,
Welcome to all, by childhood chiefly hailed,
Bringing that day the angels ushered in
O'er favoured Bethlehem; and every house
Is waked with joy, no pagan palace knew.
Now to the hearth the Christmas-log is rolled,
Huge, unassailed by severing wedge and maul:

Not the light pine, consuming in a day,
Or loud explosive chestnut whose report
Oft calls the housewife with her hurried broom;
But hickory, solid, or, more common, oak,
Whose knotted grain defies the splitting axe;
Which, once arranged, behind the andirons glows,
Devouring many a forelog, daily brought,
Till New Year rolls another in its place.
    Behold where through the starry twilight air,
Across the field, with crispy footfalls, walk
Olivia and Amy, bearing each,
From Baldwin's pantry, something for the dame
Who in the lonely Oakland shadow dwells;
While Master Ethan, in his ancient coat,
Whose long skirts sweep the snow, strides on before
Bearing the fowl—no plumper crowds the roost—
To cheer the morrow's feast. Beside her door,
Already, the rough wain has tracked the snow,
And shed the winter cord; and on the sill
The miller's frequent sack, to-day, was left.
Oh, ye, who sit in warm, penurious ease,
Did ye but know the recompense which flows,
Richer than gold, unto the heart that gives,
Your very selfishness would master self,
Till, on the coldest night of all the year,

There should not be a hearth-stone unablaze;
Or in a pantry want of wherewithal
To bless the humble board, however poor!
    The door approached, the comfortable flame
Gleams through unlisted crannies and the small
Four panes which make a window; while above
The cheerful smoke, shot through with frequent sparks,
Mounts on the still cold air. A hasty glance
They cast, and set their burthens down, and turn
To leave; when at the door, with startling voice,
The dame arrests them, crying, "Fly not so!
Stay yet awhile; for knowing who ye are,
I wot, there are some thanks for me to pay.
At least, fair damsels, let me pass my hand
A moment o'er your own; and, in the dark,
Perchance, I'll tell you something not amiss.
Oh, here is joy!" she cries—the while she draws
Her bony finger o'er Olivia's palm—
"So soon to come it needs no prophecy!"
Then, taking Amy's shrinking hand in her's,
With low, confiding voice she speaks:—"When times
Have changed, and bring to you the need of friends,
Beneath this humble roof one may you find.
Here is a shelter where the tainted breath,
The bad world loves to breathe, cannot invade:

Cold slander points not at a couch like mine.
This have the outcasts for their comfort; while
That low and horrid shed must yet be built,
Which hath not space enough for Peace to enter."
Thus having heard, they turn beyond the gate,
And leave her murmuring to herself; and soon
The farm-house takes them to its glowing arms.
How swell the young hearts round the evening board,
While spreads conjecture of the coming gifts!
And soon the stockings at the jamb
Are hung, convenient, where the promised saint,
Through sooty entrance, shall descend unseen.
Oh, thou brave, generous spirit, whose sure round
Comes yearly, like the snow—Saint Nicholas,
Or Santa Claus—or, in these sylvan vales,
"Kriss Kringle" called—of all the blessed saints
Which, as the legends say, revisit earth,
I have chief faith in thee! For thou dost come,
Noiseless and unobtrusive, to thy shrines,
The Christmas hearths; and to thy votaries givest,
And takest naught, save, at the early morn,
The countless thanks, from youthful hearts of joy,
Given in shouts profuse. In what strange form
Thou comest is not known; but fancy deems

Thy breast is swept with patriarchal beard,
Thy silver locks encased in downy cap,
Thy ample mantle of the softest furs,
Native to arctic climes; thy starry car—
Laden at Nuremberg's toy-crowded gables—
A sleigh, with silver runners, which through
Clouds of snow, unfallen on the frosty dark,
Flies drawn by spirits of a Lapland team,
With shadowy antlers broad, whose many bells
Are only heard in slumber's dreamy air.
Thus wilt thou come to-night; and, with the dawn,
Whether thou stayest to hear, or fliest afar,
To shade thy head a twelvemonth in thy realm—
Withdrawn, unknown—the happiest laughing voice
Sincerest of the year, shall swell with praise
And gratitude to thy mysterious name.
Along the valleys winds the coachman's horn,
Announcing his approach; and while his steeds
Are led to stable, steaming as they go,
And fresher are brought out, one traveller
Alights; and, straightway, favoured by the moon,
Takes the near path across, through field and grove,
And on the hill, which gives the vale to sight,
Stands for a moment, breathless with his joy.
His shadow, like his fancy, streaming far

And swiftly in advance, along the snow,
Full twice his wonted height the figure seems
Above his shade; while all his stately frame
Is glowing, throbbing with a new delight.
The landscape swims, confused, in manly tears;
The cottage lights, like wisps, unsteady shine,
Wavering, uncertain, as his steps renew.
Swiftly he glides, recalling every spot
Which sideway meets his eye; but still his gaze
Upon one lighted window firmly holds.
Now hath he neared the gate; and, trembling now,
Steals slowly to the door, while sounds within
The boisterous laugh of children. When this fades,
His heart so loudly thunders in his brain,
He cannot catch the voice he most would hear.
His hand is at the latch; but, ere it lifts,
The door, as by a spirit oped, swings wide,
And all the brightness of the light within
Falls on his noble form; and, like a ghost,
Breathless, Olivia before him stands.
The taper drops from out her loosened grasp;
She calls his name, and swoons into his arms;
And all the household echoes, "Arthur! Arthur!"

How speed the hours between those happy hearts!
What welcomes sweet! what fluent interchange

Of all which filled their separated past!
Ne'er were two dwellings waked with deeper joy,
Than are to-night the homes of the betrothed;
So deep that sleep, admiring, stands withdrawn,
Listening unseen beneath the midnight arch.
The morrow comes, and every neighbouring house
Is filled with gladness at the welcome news—
So much is Arthur held in their esteem.
And invitations, set for different nights,
Soon fill the coming week; when the full board
Is spread, with honour to the housewife's skill,
And choicest cider-casks are bid to flow,
While fruits and nuts go round. There, every eve,
The favoured lovers lead the country reel,
Where Envy, pale, abashed at her own voice,
Shrinks from the door to more ambitious halls.
And there, the frequent centre of a group,
The happy traveller, glowing with his theme,
Repeats the wonders of the sea or land,
Spreading, to the undoubting, marvelling eye,
The pictures which his rapid language paints,
Till many a listener takes his pack and staff,
Sailing imaginary seas, to climb
The visionary Alp, or stride the plain
Where history's various-coloured tents are pitched.

BOOK TWENTY-FIRST.

The winter speeds; yet, ere the spring comes in,
On many a tree which at the cross-roads stands,
And at the village tavern and the store,
And on the blacksmith's wall — in staring print,
Or in coarse written lines — unnumbered bills
Proclaim the dissolution near at hand.
There the choice farm, and stock of household wares,
Are offered, and the day of vendue set;
And, ere from off the fields the last snow melts
From crops, another than the hand which sowed
Shall in the harvest reap. The sales begin,
While Melancholy walks from door to door,
And with strange pleasure holds divided sway.
Already the great wains, with produce filled,
Have groaned their way unto the distant market,
And in return brought back such various stores

As the long journey needs—the rifle, axe,
And ammunition for defence and game;
While evening oft beholds around the hearth,
As in those days when war convulsed the land,
The molten lead run into moulded balls,
Till every pouch is full and, with the horn,
Hangs waiting on the wall. At many a door
The new-bought wagon, with its cover white,
Stands with the long tongue ready for the team.
From house to house the auction goes by turns;
While flock the people in from miles around,
And bear at eve, well pleased, the purchase home.
Thus oft the household goods, as to the winds
Blowing from fitful quarters, fly afar,
Like severed families, to meet no more;
And oft the sad wife, gazing where they go,
Needs dry the starting tear. The sales proceed;
The various round is well nigh done; and now
To Baldwin's dwelling comes the fatal day.
From loft to cellar, all the staid old house
Is made to pour its contents to the yard,
Until the feet most native to the stairs
Wake but a hollow, uncongenial sound,
Saddening, sepulchral—until each heart feels
As if the stranger, at the outer door,

Stood waiting with his wares. The brown old clock,
Slender and tall, with curious antique face,
Which stood for three-score years with hourly tongue,
Warning and cheering—or, if none would hear,
Like childish age, still garruling to itself—
Now passes silent through the mournful door,
Borne, carefully, foot first. The faithful wheels
Which, like the cat with purring voice of peace,
Sang as the flax from off the distaffs ran,
The mothers and the daughters stand outside,
Whirling to idle hands. The bureau old,
With deep and odorous drawers, where oft the rose
Scattered its leaves to scent the snow-white robes,
Is lightly thrummed upon, with careless fingers,
Or peered into, with calculating eyes,
Measuring its worth. And there the mirror tall,
Which now hath ta'en farewell of well known forms,
Reflects the stranger and the bustling scene.
See, how the crier's hard, unpitying look
Gloats o'er the medley mass, while all draw near!
Swift as a rattle flies his marvellous tongue,
While his quick eye, from face to face, darts round,
Catching the nod ere full consent approves.
And the rough joke, which wakes the crowd to mirth,
Adds a fresh blow unto the aching hearts

Of those who, piecemeal, see their home destroyed,
Part after part, as rafters to a flame,
With sound of desolation, falling in.
Among the heirlooms, note the aged pair,
Downcast as at a funeral, move about
With nervous stealth, taking a sad farewell
Of many a dumb old friend. The palsied dame
Among the curious children, shuffling, goes
From room to room, with wondering mournful eyes;
Or on the last chair, by the starving hearth,
Crouches, and gazes in the cheerless fire.
And Master Ethan, stifling many a sigh,
Affects the cheerful, and sets out the ware;
The while the matron, favouring the move,
Stirs chief amid the scene; and, frequent, chides
The tear upon Olivia's cheek, yet oft,
With hasty apron, clears her own blurred gaze.
The day goes by; the evening quiet comes,
Where sadness half way dims their one poor light,
Until, to such rough temporary beds
As haste and need can make, they seek repose:
Some dreaming of the past, and some
Of the to-morrow's busy scene—of ties
Soon to be broken, and no more renewed;
While Fancy oft, before the expedition,

Flies like the horizon, and in forest depths
Pitches the evening tent. The starting-morn,
Full of bright sunshine, bursts upon the vale;
But in the broken home—their home no more—
A stranger foot hath pressed, and led one hence,
Without a breath announcing to the air
His coming or departure; and the house,
From Master Ethan to the youngest there,
Is shadowed with a sudden gust of grief.
There lies the grandam, placid as in sleep,
Where she shall wake no more. The weary soul
Hath left its time-worn tenement of earth,
Shaking the dust from off its pilgrim feet
Against a sinful world, and passed to Heaven.
The news is spread, and all the wagons wait.
A few swift days fly o'er the dreary vale;
And, for the last time, to the chapel-yard
The pastor turns his steps, where follow, soon,
The mournful train. And now the grave is filled;
The last sad mound is shaped, as 'twere a seal
Signing the separation made in peace,
Or monument to the departing hour.

BOOK TWENTY-SECOND.

HERE, by the highway, let us stand and note
The long, slow, labouring caravan which takes,
To-day, its westward course. Like moving tents,
The laden wagons pass. Along the road
Some, who remain, collect in wayside groups,
And wave the 'kerchief, uttering heartfelt words
Of cheer; some join the pilgrimage a space,
Walking behind the wains in converse meet,
Speeding the adventurers on. Some, in advance,
Who started earlier on the way, with gaze
Cast frequent back, and leisure, mournful steps,
Hold melancholy talk with those whom they,
Perchance, shall see no more. Saddest of these,
Young Amy, leaning on her lover, walks,
Her tears usurping all her powers of speech;
While he, as voluble as spring-time brooks,

Pours in her ear the promise which her hope
Gathers and holds in its securest depths.
A few short weeks will soon go by, and then
His steps shall follow to their forest home,
Where thought of separation shall no more
Affright her tender soul. With words like these
He drowns, at last, the saddest of her fears.
On yonder height, where forks the woodland road,
And the old finger-boards with letters pale,
Long washed by storms, direct diverging ways,
The schoolhouse stands, where master Ethan taught,
Now silent as a bee-deserted hive; the shutters closed,
As on a room of death, while chain and lock
Make the lone door secure. There, on her cane,
Beneath the hand-post, stands the Oakland dame
Watching the winding line with curious eye.
When Amy passes she exalts her voice,
Waving a cautious finger as she speaks:
"Remember, lass, the words of Christmas eve!"
And, suddenly, across the young girl's heart
Flashes the whole sad sentence she then heard.
Loud laughs the youth, and bids her hold her peace;
And Amy, trembling as they pass her by,
Hastens her onward steps. Next, following, come
Olivia and Arthur; after these,

Frail Master Ethan, with his pilgrim cane,
Leading the wondering grandchild by the hand;
Then, next, the wagons. First, the well-shod team
Bearing the blacksmith's household; following this,
The wheelwright, full of magisterial pomp,
Directs his steeds, holding himself the centre
And spring of all the movement. One of those,
Chancing in front, who arrogate the lead;
Or, in the rear, is driver—nothing less.
Adverse or fair, the world from one proud point
Is viewed and met; if good, it is his due—
If ill, another's fault; yet ne'er so bad,
But that the saddest half, by skill of his,
Is headed and turned off. The ridden world
Bears many such; and oft obeys the reins,
Which arrogance usurps with shameless hand,
While modest wisdom stands aside, abashed.
There, next, the mason and the cooper come,
Their wives and children from the crowded wain
Peering abroad, with eyes half smiles and tears;
And, in communion close, the parson's team
And Baldwin's bring the rear. Anon they gain
The summit of the height, and turn to gaze;
And, gazing, heave the sigh, and breathe adieu,
While many a rough hand feels the farewell grasp.

At length the long leave-taking is all o'er;
The train descends; and lo, the happy vale
Is closed from sight beyond the mournful hill,
And all the West, before the onward troop,
Lies in the far unknown. As goes a bride,
With pain and joy alternate in her breast,
To find a home within the alien walls
Of him who hath enticed her hence—her heart
More hoping than misgiving—so, to-day,
Departed the slow train; and now the miles,
Gliding beneath with gradual but sure pace,
Bring them at last to unfamiliar scenes.
Thoughtful they hold their onward, plodding course,
Each in his own reflection wrapt; for now,
With every step, some ancient tie is broke,
Some dream relinquished, or some friend given up;
While old associations spring, self-called,
Even as tears, unbidden. Thus, awhile,
They keep the silent tenour of their way;
Till, like a sudden, unexpected bird,
Which from the still fields soars into the air,
Flooding the noon with melody, up swells
The gladsome voice of Arthur into song,
Cheering the drooping line.

"Bid adieu to the homestead, adieu to the vale,
Though the memory recalls them, give grief to the
gale:
There the hearths are unlighted, the embers are black,
Where the feet of the onward shall never turn back.
For as well might the stream that comes down from
the mount,
Glancing up, heave the sigh to return to its fount;
Yet the lordly Ohio feels joy in his breast
As he follows the sun, onward, into the West.

There the great inland seas wash their measureless
shores,
The voice of whose grandeur Niagara pours;
There the wide prairie rolls, a deep ocean, away,
Where the bison toss through in leviathan play;
Or oft pours through autumn a deluge of fire,
Where the herds fly, like demons, in fear and in ire.
At the noon or the midnight, in tempest or rest,
The sublime hath its realm in the land of the West.

Oh, to roam, like the rivers, through empires of woods,
Where the king of the eagles in majesty broods;
Or to ride the wild horse o'er the boundless domain,
And to drag the wild buffalo down to the plain;

There to chase the fleet stag, and to track the huge
bear,
And to face the lithe panther at bay in his lair,
Are a joy which alone cheers the pioneer's breast,
For the only true hunting-ground lies in the West!

Leave the tears to the maiden, the fears to the child,
While the future stands beckoning afar in the wild;
For there Freedom, more fair, walks the primeval
land,
Where the wild deer all court the caress of her hand.
There the deep forests fall, and the old shadows fly,
And the palace and temple leap into the sky.
Oh, the East holds no place where the onward can
rest,
And alone there is room in the land of the West!"

Thus swelled the song, and cheerfulness at last,
With the new scene, possess the flying hour.
And when the evening, like a tollman gray,
Drops his dusk bar across the winding road,
Before the dull, secluded wayside inn,
The laden wains collect, where tired teams
Hear the loud creaking pump, and rustling hay
Which from the near mow rolls; or dusty oats

Poured into troughs, and heave the hungry neigh.
Around the evening hearth, the cheerful groups
Collect; and, in the novel hour, forget
Their various regrets and their fatigues,
While jest and laugh go round. Alone, withdrawn,
The mournful Amy by Olivia sits;
And, on the willing shoulder of her friend,
Leans her sad head, and pours her heart of grief,
Mingled with hope, to the confiding breast
Which, having known a kindred pain, can feel,
And, feeling, give its depth of sympathy.
How beautiful is innocence which, thus,
To innocence consigns its deepest thought!—
How pure! how angel-like! A sacred scene
Which, to the brow of cold, suspecting man—
They most suspicious who betray—should start
The colour, given by the sudden blow
Of self-reproach, upon the scoundrel front.

BOOK TWENTY-THIRD.

Another morning finds them on their way:
Another still, and still another flies.
To-day beside the Susquehanna leads
Their road romantic; and to-day, the sun,
Looking betwixt the hill-tops to the vales,
Beholds, with cheerful eye, the climbing line
Which by the roaring Juniata winds;
Till lo! upon the windy mountain height,
While glows the eve above a sea of hills,
Flushing the Alleghanian peaks, the train
Hangs like a cloud that, with the coming day,
Beside the brook which takes a westward course
Shall hold its far descent. Here, from the road,
They turn into the woods beneath the pines,
And, mid the budding laurels, pitch their camp.
The wains, together, in close circle drawn,

Give shelter to the steeds that feed within.
At once, in noisy groups, all hands collect
The dry, dead branches and the resinous cones,
And build the fire, and hew the stakes and crane ;
While Master Ethan, fathoming his pouch,
Draws out the line, and Arthur trims the rod.
And soon along the wild, tumultuous brook
The bait is swept; and oft, as to the eddy
It whirls, mid spray and foam, the mountain trout
Flickers in the air its constellated sides
To eke the evening meal. The camp-fire springs,
And the red day fades out, and leaves the sky
To the cold April moon and stars — the moon,
As Ceres' sickle, thin, and sharp, and bright.
Behold where glide the dusk forms to and fro
Before the crackling blaze, their shadows far
Reaching among the pines! Throughout the night
The hungry fire is fed by those who hold,
By turns, the dreary watch — a foretaste this
Of many a night to come, in gloomy depths
Of wildernesses, far, unknown. Strange sounds
Are floating on the gusty air; the limbs,
In wavy motion, make continuous noise
As of a mighty river roaring by;
While, as night deepens, louder brawl the brooks,

Flashing their spectral light among the rocks:
One sweeping east, unto the Chesapeake—
One west, to Mississippi and the Gulf.
To such inhospitable heights as this,
Where the thin air unto the palest cheek
Sends the quick blood, the fancy deems that sleep
Would scarcely come, or, coming, stay not long;
But now in many a tented wain she sits,
Soothing the fallen lid with murmurous sounds,
Despite the young, capricious imp of dreams,
Who half way mars her choicest task. The watch
Of middle night is Arthur's; when his form
Stands tall and brave against the steadfast blaze,
One other figure steals unto his side,
And, 'gainst persuasion, shares the starry hour:
For love, more sure than sleep, attends the course
Of whosoever once hath harboured him.
Where'er they look, the black and pillared pines
Sway to and fro, as if some giant arm,
Like Samson's, rocked them to their fall; and yet
The tempest, in his oft accustomed track,
Sits, like a hunter mid his leash of hounds,
Resting, uncertain where to bend his steps.
The moon, above the shadowy mountain lines,
Drops its increasing crescent, where the hope

Of those two hearts as one together glides,
To round and brighten in the distant West.
Dear, as a new star to the wakeful eye
Of one who, on a midnight tower, keeps watch,
Is scene like this unto the tuneful muse:
The maid all tenderness and trust, and rich
With sympathies which time alone can show;
The other boundless in his guardian love,
Which colours even his most ambitious dream;—
A noble nature, full of great desires,
And whom the well-pleased future shall behold
A leader mid his people. Night departs;
The stars withdraw behind a veil of light,
To gild in other worlds the evening sky,
While morning rules in this. When now the sun,
Like a swift diver 'neath a vessel's keel,
Hath swept the nether space, and all a-glow
Exalts his shining forehead in the east—
Laying his level arms across the hills—
Gazing, delighted, where he climbs, refreshed—
The white train, like a bank of spring-time snow
Loosened by warmth, glides slowly down along
The steep and melting fords; while constant care
Scarce shuns the dread abyss which yawns beside
The freezing depths where, half the summer through,

Some straggling follower of winter rests,
Lodged in his sheltered tent of sunless snow.
Still by their side, companioning their way,
The embryo river — here a gust of foam
Which the deer leaps, and hunter, undismayed,
Seizing a rough branch, follows — headlong flies.
Days come and close; and, with another eve,
Against the sky their ken discerns, well-pleased,
The swinging cloud, starred through with meteor sparks
Which, hourly, o'er the Iron City floats,
Announcing where the loud and labouring forge
And furnace flame, continuous, throb and glow.
And when within the hospitable yards
Of well-stored inns, the teams are led ungeared,
And matrons, maids, and children, round the fire,
Thaw out the memory of the mountain cold, —
The men and youths, adventurous, sally forth,
And seek the red mouth of the furnace broad,
Where flows the iron into smoky moulds;
Or stand, admiring, where the hammer huge
Falls on the white hot metal, at each blow
Filling the space with sudden rain of fire;
Or how the hungry rollers take the mass,
And yield, at length, the long and slender bars.
Here Barton stands, as native to the scene,

And feels the impulse of his noble craft
Thrill to his fingers, with a fond desire
To grasp the bar and sledge. The morning comes:
Behold where noisy builders by the stream,
With axe and adze, construct the future arks,
To sweep the Ohio to its mouth, and take
The Mississippi, in its swift career,
Wide-winding 'twixt the boundaries of States
As lesser streams 'twixt farms. Here, on this beam,
The fresh-hewn poplar, which among its fellows
Sweetens the air with odours, till it floats
Enamoured in the sun as o'er a garden,
Let us sit down, unstartled—sit and hear
The song of labour, whose resounding blow
Sounds like a voice proclaiming to the future
The march of this, our forward-going age.
The song of labour! nobler song is not!
He is the bard who writes, in living acts,
The epic of the era; every stroke
A word prophetic of the great hereafter.
Observe this group of workmen who prepare
The beams and boards, and clear the ample space,
To shape the flat-boat's square, ungraceful form.
Some line and score, and with the broad-axe hew
The giant log: and then the whip-saw comes,

Long, slender, biting as a champion's sword,
And double-handled, manned at either end,
One on the up-reared trunk and one beneath!
See how the swift blade, as the lightning, flies,
Severing, like death, what time can never join!
Thus separated, and the ends a-slope,
Hewn equal, like the runners of a sleigh—
Huge as a northern army might desire,
To bear provisions for a winter camp—
They upturned lie; and now the oaken planks
Reach crosswise, pinned and spiked from end to end.
Then, with dull chisel, and the noisy mallet,
The swingling-tow is driven into the seams,
Till all are caulked, and comes the black cement,
Of molten odorous pitch, which gives secure
Protection 'gainst invasion of the wave.
Anon, the monster hull, by levers reared,
Heaves a great vault in air, and righted thus,
Lies ready for the launch. The rails are laid,
And to the slippery slope the boat is given;
And, lo! the wooden avalanche descends
Sheer to the middle of the stream, to be
Recalled by checking cables. As it strikes,
One, mid loud shouts from the resounding shore,
Breaks on the bow the deep baptismal flask;

And let our hopes with his be freely joined,
With heartfelt prayers that fair Prosperity
May spread her pinions o'er the sailor's ark;
For this the deck which Providence ordains
To bear our travellers hence. A few swift days
Go by: the boat is covered, and complete
Within and out. On either side the oars,
And one astern, from ashen sapling hewn—
Each suppled, toughened many seasons through
In sweeping rivers of the mountain wind—
Droop, like unfolded wings, half spread for flight.
And now, in groups, unto the crowded wharf
The various households gather with their wares,
And soon betake them to their floating home;
And, drawn in close assemblies on the deck,
Gaze, wondering, at the tumult which they leave;
Bidding adieu to Pennsylvanian shores,
Which few, of all the crowd, shall tread again.
When, suddenly, a well-known voice is heard,
And all, delighted, hearken as it swells:

"Lo, our waiting ark is freighted;
In its depths of oak and pine
All our household goods are gathered—
Thine, my noble friend, and mine!

Here the laughter-loving children
  Gaze, with wonder-filling eyes,
With the maidens whose emotions,
  Like the waters, fall and rise.

Here are youths whose westward fancies
  Chase the forest-sheltered game;
Here are men with soul and sinew
  Which no wilderness can tame.

Here are matrons, full of courage—
  Worthy these the pioneers—
And the patriarch lends a sanction
  In the wisdom of his years.

Axe and team, and plough and sickle,
  In the hold are gathered all;
And, methinks, I hear the woodlands,
  Mid their thundering echoes, fall.

And behold the great logs blazing.
  Till the ashen fields are bare,
And a boundless harvest springing—
  The response of toil and prayer!

Draw the foot-board, loose the cables,
  Free the wharf, and man the oars;
Give the broad keel to the river,
  Bid adieu to crowded shores:

Wharves where Europe's venturous exiles
  Throng with all their hopes and cares—
Sires of future States of freemen,
  Standing mid their waiting wares.

Bid adieu the Iron City,
  With its everlasting roar,
Whose Niagara of traffic
  Flows to westward evermore.

Where the cloud swings into heaven,
  And the furnace flames disgorge,
With the multitudinous clamour
  Of the factory and the forge.

In yon mountains, like the eagles,
  Brood the rivers at their springs,
Then descend, with sudden swooping,
  On their far and flashing wings.

Here the dashing Alleghany
  And Monongahela meet,
And a moment whirl and dally
  Round the city's crowded feet;

Till, anon, with wedded pinions,
  How they sweep the shores as one,
Driving westward, ever westward,
  In the pathway of the sun.

Like a cloud upon the storm-wind,
  Now our heaving ark careers;
Or some great bridge which a freshet
  Bears in triumph from its piers.

Down we sweep; and yonder steamer
  Smoking round the distant hill,
With its swift wheel flashing splendour,
  Like the loud wheel of a mill,

Shall not fright us, though the waters
  Sweep our deck with foamy force,
While the angel of Adventure,
  With true courage, guides our course.

And the river, like our purpose,
  Brooks no voice which bids it wait,
Bearing onward, ever onward,
  Where the forest opes its gate;

Opes the gate that hung for ages,
  Rusting in its old repose,
Which, once swung upon its hinges,
  There's no giant hand can close.

Far beyond that ancient portal
  We will pitch our camp, nor rest
Till from out our forest cabins
  Spring the homesteads of the West."

BOOK TWENTY-FIFTH.

Between the hills whose perforated sides
Bleed to the watered banks, from veins of coal,
The black bituminous mass, for days they float
Delighted with the changing view. The shore,
On either hand, a lovely landscape glides:
And Beaver passed, lo, presently appear
The fields of other States. Here, on the left,
Virginia, whose historic name recalls
The scenes of chivalry and old romance—
A State which lavished heroes, as a mountain
Gives to the land its rivers. The broad home
Of Raleigh's hope and Pocahontas' love,
Of Washington and Jefferson, and him
Who, midst the cry of "treason," shook the world,
Till tyranny, with all his traitor band,
A-pace recoiled as billows to the blast.

There on the right, behold, more newly freed
From the grim forest's grasp, the lovely land
Christened in honour of the stream which bears
The produce of her fruitful farms afar.
    The time arrives when labour's iron doors
Are closed upon the tumult of the week,
Secure, as evening shuts behind the day;
And, when the silent hour is ushered in,
A dusky island on the river looms,
Brooding above its shadow, like a cloud
Bereft of all the winds—companionless,
It hangs suspended o'er the inverted sky,
Concealing half the river stars. And here
The heavy ark unto the sheltering shore
Glides noiseless, as an eagle swooping in
To rest beneath the over-arching limbs,
And soon the cables hold it to the bank
Among the watery willows. In the east,
As red and wide as is the forge's mouth
Oft seen mid Alleghanian hills, the moon—
Like some great soul, a-flush with earthly lusts,
That nobly rises from its base estate—
Ascends, each moment lessening from the stain,
Until the heavens receive it pure and white.
Invited by her ray, unto the shore

The lovers wander through the sinuous paths,
In happy freedom from the crowded deck,
And Arthur to Olivia repeats
The saddening tale of Blennerhassett's isle:

"Once came an exile, longing to be free,
Born in the greenest island of the sea;
He sought out this, the fairest blooming isle
That ever gemmed a river; and its smile,
Of summer green and freedom, on his heart
Fell, like the light of Paradise. Apart
It lay, remote and wild; and in his breast
He fancied this an island of the blest;
And here he deemed the world might never mar
The tranquil air with its molesting jar.
Long had his soul, among the strife of men,
Gone out and fought, and, fighting, failed; and then
Withdrew into itself: as when some fount
Finds space within, and will no longer mount,
Content to hear its own secluded waves
Make lonely music in the new-found caves.
And here he brought his household; here his wife,
As happy as her children, round his life
Sang as she were an echo, or a part
Of the deep pleasure springing in his heart—

A silken string which with the heavier cord
Made music, such as well-strung harps afford.
She was the embodied spirit of the man,
His second self, but on a fairer plan.
And here they came, and here they built their home,
And set the rose and taught the vines to roam,
Until the place became an isle of bowers,
Where odours, mist-like, swam above the flowers.
It was a place where one might lie and dream,
And see the naiads, from the river-stream,
Stealing among the umbrous, drooping limbs;
Where Zephyr, mid the willows, tuned her hymns
Round rippling shores. Here would the first birds
throng,
In early spring-time, and their latest song
Was given in autumn; when all else had fled,
They half forgot to go; such beauty here was spread.
It was, in sooth, a fair enchanted isle,
Round which the unbroken forest, many a mile,
Reached the horizon like a boundless sea;—
A sea whose waves, at last, were forced to flee
On either hand, before the westward host,
To meet no more upon its ancient coast.
But all things fair, save truth, are frail and doomed;
And brightest beauty is the first consumed

By envious Time; as if he crowned the brow
With loveliest flowers, before he gave the blow
Which laid the victim on the hungry shrine:—
Such was the dreamer's fate, and such, bright isle,
was thine.
There came the stranger, heralded by fame,
Whose eloquent soul was like a tongue of flame,
Which brightened and despoiled whate'er it touched.
A violet, by an iron gauntlet clutched,
Were not more doomed than whosoe'er he won
To list his plans, with glowing words o'errun:
And Blennerhassett hearkened as he planned.

Far in the South there was a glorious land,
Crowned with perpetual flower, and where repute
Pictured the gold more plenteous than the fruit—
The Persia of the West. There would he steer
His conquering course; and o'er the bright land rear
His far-usurping banner, till his home
Should rest beneath a wide, imperial dome,
Where License, round his throned feet, should whirl
Her dizzy mazes like an orient girl.
His followers should be lords; their ladies each
Wear wreaths of gems beyond the old world's reach;
And emperors, gazing to that land of bloom,
With impotent fire of envy should consume.

Such was the gorgeous vision which he drew.
The listener saw; and, dazzled by the view—
As one in some enchanter's misty room,
His senses poisoned by the strange perfume,
Beholds with fierce desire the picture fair,
And grasps at nothing in the painted air—
Gave acquiescence, in a fatal hour,
And wealth, and hope, and peace were in the tempter's power.
The isle became a rendezvous; and then
Came in the noisy rule of lawless men.
Domestic calm, affrighted, fled afar,
And Riot revelled 'neath the midnight star.
Continuous music rustled through the trees,
Where banners danced responsive on the breeze;
Or in festoons, above the astonished bowers,
With flaming colours shamed the modest flowers.
There clanged the mimic combat of the sword,
Like daily glasses round the festive board;
Here lounged the chiefs, there marched the plumed file,
And martial splendour over-run the isle.
Already, the shrewd leader of the sport
The shadowy sceptre grasped, and swayed his court.
In dream, or waking, revelling or alone,
Before him swam the visionary throne;

Until a voice, as if the insulted woods
Had risen to claim their ancient solitude,
Broke on his spirit, like a trumpet rude,
Shattering his dream to nothing as he stood!
The revellers vanished, and the banners fell,
Like the red leaves beneath November's spell.
Full of great hopes, sustained by mighty will,
Urged by ambition, confident of skill,
As fearless to perform as to devise,
A-flush, but now he saw the glittering prize
Flame like a cloud in day's descending track;
But, lo, the sun went down, and left it black!
Alone, despised, defiance in his eye,
He heard the shout, and "treason!" was the cry;
And that harsh word, with its unpitying blight,
Swept o'er the island like an arctic night.
Cold grew the hearthstone, withered fell the flowers,
And desolation walked among the bowers.

This was the mansion. Through the ruined hall
The loud winds sweep, with gusty rise and fall,
Or glide, like phantoms, through the open doors;
And winter drifts his snow along the floors,
Blown through the yawning rafters, where the stars
And moon look in as through dull prison bars

On yonder gable, through the nightly dark,
The owl replies unto the dreary bark
Of lonely fox, beside the grass-grown sill;
And here, on summer eves, the whip-poor-will
Exalts her voice, and to the traveller's ear
Proclaims how ruin rules with full contentment here."

BOOK TWENTY-SIXTH.

Thus sang the poet-lover, mid the scenes
Where happiness once brooded like a dove.
The mournful tale is ended with a sigh,
And she who listened weeps; and where they stand
The sad moon ponders, like the ghost of Eve
All night a-gazing on an Eden lost.
The conjuring fancy fills the place with shapes,
Holding their doubtful tryste; the o'ershadowed eye
Peoples the dusk with phantoms; and the ear,
By keen imagination finely tuned,
Like a light cord to fullest tension drawn,
Vibrates to each accordant sigh of air,
And hears a world of sounds, where ruder sense
Would only note the silence. Did you hear?
Was it a rustle in the budding limbs,
Or lone bird darting from his wakeful branch?

Did you not see?—There, through the light, and there!
Was it a spirit swept across their path?
And hark again! a sound as of a wave,
Weary of rolling to a pitiless wind,
Dashing its tired breast against a rock!
Near by, the river reels around a point,
Sweeping from darkness into sudden light—
So near, the lovers' slanting shadows glide,
Bending together, o'er the dreamy bank.
An instant Arthur gazes on the stream,
And bounds aside, and leaps into the flood,
And bears a dripping figure to the shore;
While, like a marble wonder, speechless stands
The pale Olivia: even as one in sleep,
Who fain would follow while the feet, enchained,
Refuse their wonted office. On his arm
The deluged form, with loosened, oozing locks,
Hangs, like a sea-nymph, fainting; from her face,
Which to the moon's astonishment gives back
A look of pallid sorrow, the hair smoothed,
Displays the well-known features of their friend.
Olivia, frighted, bends above the form,
And calls her "Amy! Amy!" till the ear,
Dulled with the water, hears, and the sad eyes,
Bewildered, ope, as if to meet the shapes

And scenes of other worlds—amazed, confused,
Uncertain if an angel speaks her name,
Or if a spirit bears her soul released.
Conscious, at last, she clasps her bosom-friend,
And sighs "forgive, forgive!" Sad heart, she feels
The weight of crime attempted, yet scarce knows—
So tangled, like a delicate web, her brain—
'Gainst whom or what! But e'er the night is o'er,
While sits Olivia by the cabin couch,
The sole receiver of her inmost thought—
In concert to the under-going stream
Which, like the river of death, flows darkly near—
She pours upon the sympathizing breast
Her deep heart-drowning sorrow and her fears;
And both, together, weep the long night through,
Or pray in union while their comrades sleep.
    Oh, Heaven, if e'er thy pitying angel stoops,
As holiest faith believes, and in the hour
Of fear and pain breathes his consoling voice,
Like sounds of waters to the ear of one
Who droops in deserts lone—in this sad place
Permit his wings to fold beside the couch,
And bid him shed into the fainting soul
The holy calm whence courage only springs!
The world is full of sadness: oft the smile

16

Is but the flower, above decaying hopes,
Blooming to hide a ruin. But a sight,
Saddest of all — sadder than sudden death —
It is to see a young heart touched with frost,
And all its freshness scattered to the wind; —
A heart which had been full of joy, all hope,
All love, all trust, break from its hold of all,
And, like an easy, noiseless bank of sand,
Fall, crumbling by continuous degrees,
Into the gulfy river of despair.

BOOK TWENTY-SEVENTH.

ADIEU the island! Lo, the Sabbath dawns,
A cloudless April-day. Still toward the West
The broad stream bears them onward in its arms.
On either shore, and through the neighbouring fields,
While sounds the bell from yonder village spire,
The unknown people throng. Then to the deck
The various inmates of the ark collect,
And round the pastor drawn, in pious groups,
Flood the calm air with the melodious hymn;
While, as they pass the town, an answer comes,
Like a clear echo, from the hill-side church.
The melody into their hearts descends—
The old familiar tune—till every breast
Is waked to joy, and even the sternest eye
Is moistened with a sympathizing mist.

How beautiful, in such an hour and place,
To hear from stranger lips, unseen perchance,
That never may be seen till met in Heaven,
The sacred sounds proclaiming brotherhood—
The masonry of souls! How beautiful!
In all the world of art—a wondrous world—
I know no picture lovelier than to-day
Melts o'er my vision. Chief amid the group—
A dwindled portion of his former flock—
Each face familiar, all, as children, dear—
The pastor stands, and on his loving arm
Holds the great volume, and, with sunburnt hand,
Turns o'er the intimate leaves. Ope where he will,
The broad page greets him like a well-known friend.
Near by, with white hair stirring to the breeze,
Frail Master Ethan, leaning on his cane,
Stands hat in hand. The matrons, on the deck,
Sit with the children at their careful sides;
There youths and maids respectful posture hold;
And every man draws near, save those who lean
And listen at the easy moving oars.

Suns rise and set, and still the boat glides on;
Peace rules the day, and music cheers the eve.
Lo, on the south extends the lovely land
Where strode the solitary man of old,

Bursting upon the entangled night of woods,
Like prophecy, proclaiming where he went
The forest's fall, and the red man's decline!
Here the lone Nimrod of the pathless West
Reigned with his rifle, and, through hostile wilds,
Won to himself an empire undisturbed.
His nights o'erhung with royal tents of limbs,
His vernal board with venison was crowned,
His cup with coolest crystal from the rocks;
And oft unto his morning throne of state—
A crag which overbrowed the stateliest woods—
He mounted, and surveyed his wide domain,
Deciding where to bend his further sway.
Behind him, like the murmuring of the sea
Which, to a constant wind, invades the shore,
He heard the encroaching tumult of the world;
And, with the sun, strode on a few swift miles,
Usurping, westward, what he eastward lost.
Such was the realm of Boone, the pioneer,[4]
Whose statue, in the eternal niche of fame,
Leans on his gleaming rifle; and whose name
Is carved so deep in the Kentuckian rocks,
It may not be effaced. His glorious soul,
Heroic among kindred hero souls,
Now threads the boundless forest of the stars;

While still his memory, like a spirit, walks
With living influence in his favourite land.
What means this sudden swelling of the stream,
As if a thousand springs within its depths
Had burst, like mighty geysers, to exalt
The river's watery head that, rising, roars,
And frights the banks until they swoon and drown?
Answer, ye nymphs, from out your turbid caves!
For nymphs there are in this unclassic flood,
Born of the savage muse in vanished years,
Who peopled all the solitude with shapes,
Whose spiritual whispers in the wind,
The waters and the woods, still charm the ear.
A poesy, unwritten, floats abroad,
So wide dis-spread, the echo-waking axe
Shall not dispel it; nor the busy plow
Turn it beneath the furrows; nor the train,
Thundering along its iron way, affright;
Nor smoking barges, with their flashing wheels,
Dislodge it from the waters. Every brook
And tree, could we but comprehend the song,
Is musical with voices not its own;
An influence of the primal time still lives,
And breathes, and moulds us in our daily walks,
And thus developes in us, unaware,

A something of the earliest things which were.
'Tis this which links us with the perfect plan,
The chain which was, and is, and is to be.
Even where I gaze, the fancy, in the stream,
Pictures dim, liquid shapes which rise and sink,
And sway in waves that ripple to the shore,
Intoxicate in the redundant flood.
There curved an arm, and there a bright face laughed,
With momentary eyes and lips disclosed,
And sound of sinless kisses thrown, perchance,
From watery fingers to the youths on deck.
There swim the children of the Indian muse,
Who ply at night the shadowy canoe,
While kindred forms, along the moon-lit woods,
Startle the phantom deer and wake the chase,
From whence their sires have gone—forever gone.
The man has fled, the spirit still remains—
The substance less substantial than the shade—
And still the river's sullied waters swell,
Augmented by the melting mountain snows,
And plenteous April-rains. Afar and near,
The swift careering drift chaotic flies,
Borne on the thievish shoulders of the flood!
Great trees, whirled ruthless from their native banks,
Sweep headlong, with their budding limbs all drowned,

And roots fantastic raking through the air.
These are the shapes that in the channel depths
Of Mississippi lodge—the downward prongs
Mining the sandy bed—the dreadful trunk
Swaying aslant to gore the freighted ark.
Here float the logs of some disjointed raft,
And there the woodman's scattered cords! Enough
Swims prodigal to build a nation's navy.
At such a time as this, the wary crew
Must needs, with well manned oars, avoid the drift,
While many a danger lies engulphed, unseen.
And when the night comes on, as now it comes,
And threatening clouds impend from east to west,
While all the watery shore no harbour gives,
With what misgivings, doubting hopes and fears,
The venturous watchers ride into the dark,
Where Providence assumes the swaying helm.
Loud sweeps the torrent; but with louder voice
Roars on the shoreless ocean of the wind,
Bearing the dusky navies of the storm,
Whose signal cannons, flashing, threat the land.
Along the hills gleam scattered cottage-lights,
Mocking the homeless households where they float,
Compassed with dangers which the starless night,
With cruel kindness, veils. The startled sense,

For every peril hid, beholds, thrice told,
The horror painted on the blackened air;
While oft the fancy, drowning with the wreck,
Dies momentary deaths. The grinding drifts
Chafe hoarsely at their thin and creaking walls
With frightful discord, and the ominous waves
Dash at the wide partition, as in scorn,
Striking with multitudinous hands. The lights,
Before and aft, dispense their scanty rays—
How spectral, thin, and ineffectual!—
Which oft the sheeted lightning in the south,
With sudden brilliance dims, and shows the guard,
An instant, where to set the helm and where
To ply the sidelong oar. Thus speeds the ark;
And midnight rules the wild tempestuous hour.
On deck the men are gathered by the oars;
Below, the women sit in dreary groups,
Waiting and listening: some with infants clasped,
Convulsive, on the breast, while at their feet
The older children crowd, their terror drowned
In unrecording sleep. But hark! the shock!
The shout above! the shriek below! the neigh
Of frighted steeds! Fear rules the scene. On deck
All crowd with straining eyes, which nought discern
Save random lights on shore. Their course is stopped;

And, lo, a noon-like sheet of lightning flames,
And shows their ark 'mong rafts and steamers lodged;
While, like a vision in delirium seen,
A midnight city, with its sudden spires,
Springs on their sight—a marvelous instant springs—
Then vanishes in night, and leaves them nought
But wild conjecture which must wait the dawn.
　　The storm is past; a cloudless day awakes,
And to the wondering multitudes on deck
A glorious city spreads its welcoming arms—
The Queen Metropolis of inland States—
Which, like a mighty heart, receives and gives,
Swelling through all the body of the land
The pulsing veins of trade. In foundry yards
Loud hammers ring upon the boilers huge—
Too oft the ominous knell of future deaths,
Wrought by destruction in the sudden air,
Making a murderous gap a nation feels.
In each great bolt, 'twixt double sledges clinched,
What lives are wedged—a life for every blow!
Bold wielder! strike again, and still again,
Lest that the careless stroke hereafter fall,
With triple weight, on many an aching heart!
Along the sloping wharf the giant keels
Swing by their cables, e'en as monsters chained,

Frighting the sky with hot discordant breath,
Heaved from their lungs of fire; and noisy Toil
Lays his brown shoulders to the southern bale,
Or rolls the cask ashore, where Commerce stands
Smiling among the mountainous freight, and sends
Her northern product back. Time was, my friend—
Thou, who beneath thy own Catawba vine[5]
Sittest, like autumn in a plenteous land,
Crowned with the fruits of heavy labours past,
Forgetting not thy reapers, nor the poor
Gleaning amid the stubble—when thy feet
Here paced the sod primeval, while the trees
Stretched their defiant branches unalarmed.
Then were yon hills—which now the reaching streets,
Audacious, climb with all a city's din—
Templed within a Sabbath shade of woods;
And where the eagle, on the topmost limb,
Gazed at the sun unstartled, nightly, now,
In its high tower, the astronomic glass
Sweeps the blue space to mightier suns than ours.
Within thy memory, on this self-same ground,
A forest and a giant city stand.

When now the day discloses all the scene—
The thronging wharf and their own ark half wrecked—
The adventurers hold a solemn council hour,

And in the small republic, on the deck,
Discuss their future course. Some, unapalled,
Call for repairs, impatient to be on;
Some urge a transfer to the rapid bark,
Whose flashing wheels shall bear them quickly through.
But they, whose hands grew brown upon the plough,
And they who joyed to drive the well-fed team
And laden wain to market, once more sigh
To feel the solid earth beneath their feet,
To wind their way 'twixt farms and thorough woods,
Hewing, if need be, their own forest-path.
This plan is carried; and their various wagons
Are rolled ashore, and the delighted steeds,
Pawing the ground, receive the accustomed gears,
The collar and the rein; and all, well-pleased,
Assume their places, and take up their march.
The suburbs now, and now the hills, receive
The winding line; and soon amid the fields,
The city lost, they note the stretching road
Inviting on and on. Another State,
With noble farms usurping glorious woods,
Now bids them welcome, and still cheers their course;
While, day by day, the sidelong forests grow
To longer stretches, and the new-made fields,
Rougher with fallen logs and girdled trunks,
Occur less frequent with their lessening homes.

BOOK TWENTY-EIGHTH.

WHERE a far prairie pours its yearly flood
Of verdure to a forest's dusky foot,
And where a stream to Mississippi flows
In endless vassalage; and where the beaver,
Like the red Indian and the buffalo,
Flying before the fast-encroaching plow,
The sickle and the mill, hath fled so late,
Scared by the trapper from his watery door—
While his small homestead, in the liquid plain,
With empty threshold looks abroad amazed—
And where the breastwork still retards the stream,
To hint and aid the future miller's dam;
Where, through the woodland depth, the wild deer's
track
Still shows the hoof-prints leading to the brink,
And, on the opposing shore, the larger path

Worn by the prairie herds athirst; behold
One small, rude hut of bark and motley skins
Sits, like a tired hunter, on the bank,
Companionless and still. Half drawn ashore,
A rough canoe lies dreaming; and, near by,
The forest Selkirk, sitting with his dog,
Fondles his rifle and resets the flint.
He is of those who, like the venturous bees,
Herald the nation following in their wake—
An advance courier of a world of men—
A scout, from civilization's onward line,
Sent to inspect the forest's savage camp.
Silent he muses, and, athwart his brow,
Thoughts and their shadows pass like autumn-clouds.
Perchance he walks, in the departed years,
Along some green New England vale,—a child,
Led by a parent, while his happy heart
Throbs, like an echo, to the Sabbath bell.
Dear faces rise, and loving voices speak;
A mother's hand smooths back his boyish hair;
A sister's glowing arms are round his neck;
Or, later, through the scented hay-field strolls,
Or sits beside the rose-embowered door,
With one whose snowy garment past his soul
Now rustles like an angel's floating robe.

Perchance—but no; his rough and sunburnt hand
Dashes the vision from his half-blurred gaze;
His swift eye sweeps the prairie to its verge,
And, like an arrow, darts through umbrous woods,
Where desolation owns him for its lord.

Hark! is't a panther leaping through the limbs?
Or wild buck flying from pursuit of wolves?
Or steeds, which never knew the curb of rein,
Neighing along the prairie? 'Tis a sound
Unusual to his startled ear. The dog
Recoils unto his master's feet, and listens.
But soon the accustomed eye discerns the cause;
And on the trapper's gaze the obnoxious gleam,
From the white covers of approaching wains,
Strikes on his spirit, like the light of ghosts,
Seen in a long abhorrent train. His soul
Shrinks from the vision, and within him cries:
"Is there no shelter from the reach of men?
Or must I, like the westward-going game,
Lie down in fear, and only wake to fly?
Or, like the tired courser of the plain,
Yield me unto the lasso, and submit
To wear the rein, and feel the daily whip
Which civilization wields, and be a slave
Where I have been so free? Or lay my hand

Against this brotherhood of trees, and be,
At last, a traitor to the wilderness?"
Sullen he stands, and notes the line approach;
And when a shout goes up among the limbs,
"Here will we pitch our camp and build our homes,"
He tears the prop from 'neath his cabin roof,
And from the ruin takes his load of skins,
Shoves his canoe from shore, and, with his dog,
Glides o'er the silent waters out of sight.

BOOK TWENTY-NINTH.

WHEN comes the eve — and in these antique woods
Eve comes before its time, and the deep night
With double darkness falls — then springs the blaze
Of crackling camp-fires; while the astonished trees,
Half-lighted, stand and murmur their surprise
To others crowding in the shade behind;
And many a bird with fascinated wonder,
And stealthy beast, with wide unwinking stare
And fixed amazement, gaze with silent fear,
Till night is robbed of half its dreary noise.
There stands the pastor mid his little flock,
And opes the wonted volume; while beside,
Young Arthur holds the flaming torch of pine,
Where all draw round and hearken till the close.
Then suddenly the evening hymn is given,
Thrilling the leaves with pleasure where it floats,

And, for the first, this ancient forest hears
The melody of well-accorded souls
Breathing of Christian peace; while desolation,
Pained with prophetic music, stands withdrawn,
Like some lone Indian, last of all his tribe,
Drooping his unstrung bow. Then prayer
And silence rules the camp. Near by—perchance
An arrow-shot beyond—there is a rock
Which overlooks the stream; the ripples break
About its giant foot, and from its brow
The light vines, growing many a season down,
Trail their long fingers o'er the shadowy pool.
To gain its top, and wait the rising moon,
Which, large and flaming as a chariot-wheel,
Now rolls among the eastern stars, with joy
The lovers pass, and muse upon the scene.
And fancy tells how this exalted spot
Hath been, in its oblivion of years,
The happy altar where young love hath tamed
The savage heart, until the wild soul felt
The tranquil pleasure which 'tis ours to know
Beside the Christian hearth. Or here, perchance,
In desperate hour, some Indian maid, forlorn,
Hath to the midnight flung her streaming hair,—
Plunged, like the pleiad, to be known no more.

Around, below, the world is silent, dark,
Or waked by wild, uncomprehended sounds,
Making the solitude more lone; as when
Some star-led watcher, on a noiseless deck,
Hears the far waves communing with themselves.
Speechless they rest, and gaze into the sky
On that white path of splendour, like the track
Left by a vessel on the midnight sea—
Foamy, phosphorent, nebulous and strange—
The highway of the universe, perchance,
And populous with mightier worlds than this.
From out the dusk of that deep silent wood,
They pore upon the heavens with wandering thought—
More 'wildered as it wanders through the maze
And intricate bright tangle of the stars—
Until each soul recoils into itself,
Amazed, confounded, shrinking with a sigh,—
Which sigh, interpreted aright, proclaims
"How great, eternal, boundless and sublime!
And we, how frail and insignificant!—
The merest dust upon the wings of time,
Which a rude breath, or the destroyer's finger,
Dislodges, and we pass and know not where!"
Oh, man, in thy most proud and pompous hour—
Or in the feast among the costly bowls—

Or throned upon ambition's dizzy top,
Where slaves, unto your slightest bidding, fly
As leaves before a gust—go boldly forth,
And look upon the silence of the stars;
And though your frame be armoured up in gold,
Your great soul mailed in pride, their quiet light
Shall dwindle you to nothing where you stand;
Your arrogant spirit be a point so small,
That you shall tremble lest that God's own eye
Shall not discern you, fluttering in the dust,
And leave you there, eternally forgot!
But where two souls are, and, with love between,
Not self-reliant all; but each on each
Leaning reciprocal, and both on God;
Not long the gloom of the primeval wood,
Or the profounder melancholy shade
Pervading space, can overveil their hearts:
For so divine a sentiment is theirs,
The soul dilates where others only shrink,
And, as with angels' eyes, sees all things through
The mellow, purple light of Paradise,
Making a dawn where others feel the dark.

BOOK THIRTIETH.

BEHOLD the morn! and now begins the toil.
The first loud axe alarms the forest's shade;
And there the first tree falls, and falling wide,
With spreading arms that tear their downward way
Strips the adjacent branches; the loud crash
Thunders to Heaven, and the astonished sun
Looks down the murderous gap. Thus, ever thus,
In the community of men, a wrong
To one deals injury to many more.
Hark, how the roar runs echoing through the woods,
And every oldest oak and sycamore
Thrills with prophetic feeling of its fall.

Now marks each labourer his future home;
And wheresoe'er a spring gives out its rill,
There grows the first rude temporary hut—
Named, in the language of the pioneer,

"The half-faced camp"—of hurried saplings built,
And bound by withes of vines, and roofed with bark.
In open air the steaming cauldrons swing,
While the blue smoke sweeps up among the limbs,
Tangled, impeded; where, far over all,
The forest eagle, circling, sails amazed.
Some on the prairie stake their future hearths,
Crossing the river at its nearest ford;—
There, where the crystal o'er the pebbles slides,
Leaving the imprint of the earliest wheels
Which ever pressed these cool, delicious sands.
Days come and go: at every break of dawn—
While yet the gibbous moon, above the west,
Hangs like a ghostly fragment of white cloud—
The youths are forth to find the forest game;
And oft the prairie to the woodland gives
The rifle's shrill alarm; and many a morn,
Ere the red sun hath climbed his first slant hour,
The dun deer from the bended shoulder falls,
Prone, at the cabin door. Still sounds the axe.
For many weeks the heavy forests fall,
And, falling, groan aloud, and, groaning, die;
And, dying, yield their vernal souls in smoke,
And sink in crumbled ashes to the ground,
Which the rough plow, among the jagged roots

Oft stalled, with difficult progress turns beneath
The black and antique mould. And now behold
The various crops are sown, and in the soil
Await the genial rain and summer sun,
To swell the primal harvest of the land.
This done, the pioneer may breathe a day;
And, looking round him, choose a fitter spot
To rear his home and plant his cabin ground.
Then follows trimming of the fallen logs;
The hewing, and the rolling into place,
Occasion oft of many a festive scene,
When come the neighbours, each with axe or team,
Accomplishing, by well concerted strength,
In one short day a heavy season's task.
Behold, even now, upon the gentle slope,
And near this spring which, from its rocky urn,
Pours down a runnel through a bed of moss,
The wooden dwelling must be reared to-day,
And Baldwin points the spot. With axe, and adze,
And sledge, and iron bar, and voices glad,
The labourers come, and make the toil a play.
Some place the trunks, while others notch, and hew,
And fit the ends, until, with log on log,
The walls ascend—at either corner manned—
Until, at last, against the evening sky

They stand complete, and, in the golden sun,
The mounted toilers glow like sentinels
Upon a tower of old; and now the eve,
With mirth and music filled, concludes the scene.
Thus, while the crops are springing, spring the homes,
And ruder garners for the winter store,
Till lo, a village smiles along the stream;
And all the air, with odours of the wood
Fresh-hewn, o'erfloods the place with redolence,
Sweeter than winds from the magnolian isles.
　　Gratefully to the ear the various sounds
Of pastoral life discourse: the lowing kine,
The neighing steeds, and early-crowing cocks—
Which, like clear silver bells, awake the dawn—
The only bells which mark the forest hours,
Till, hark! the smith's half-sheltered anvil rings,
And the light sparkles star the morning dusk.
And there the wheelwright rolls his first stout wheel
To take the burning tires; while at the stream,
Where toiled the beaver, lo, the breastwork grows,
And whistling builders labour mid their logs.
Here, in the pleasant sunny afternoons,
Old Master Ethan takes his little flock;
And in the shade of one great forest tree,
Left to embower the parson's summer door,

On new-fallen timber seats them round, and there
Sets up the moderate by-laws of his school.
And the low murmur of the urchins' lips
Floats on the air, commingling with the sound
Of whispering leaves that flicker overhead;
And, when the task is done, with rod and line
He strolls the woods along the sunset stream.

Ere many weeks go by, still other trains,
Fresh-breathing of the East, arrive, and fright
The farther forest with the flashing axe.
There, foremost in the crowd to welcome them,
Pale Amy stands, with disappointed gaze,
And sadly questions every newest comer,
If he has seen or heard, upon the road,
Aught of a youthful wagoner or horseman,
Hailing from Hazelmead, and bound this way.
And oft the shaken head, or careless "No,"
Strikes through her eye or ear, until her heart
Tolls in her bosom like a bell of death.
Lo! once again, upon that starlit rock,
Where there shall come no smiling moon to-night;
For she is gone beyond her wonted veil,
Gone to her monthly cloister of deep shade,
To clear her brow, in silent penitence,
Of painful memories of nightly ills

Which she beheld on earth.—Lo, once again,
And e'en the stars seem shrinking in the blue;
And o'er the prairie's unreflecting waves
The black south-west exalts its stormy wings,
And the hot light, fanned from those gusty vans,
Darts up the sky in sudden, transient dawns;
While o'er the stream, and o'er the sultry grass,
The myriad fire-flies mimic the far cloud.—
Lo, once again; but not the tranquil scene,
Where love led fancy in a wildered maze,
Through constellated gardens in the blue;
But holier, if holier can be.
Step lightly; for 'tis God's deep, chastening sorrow
Usurps the hour, and fills its solemn task.
Two forms are there; and one, with posture prone,
Hides her sad face upon the other's lap.
"I wait, and wait, and yet he will not come;
My mother chides me for my fruitless grief;
My father frowns upon me at his board;
Oh, better I had died before I loved!
Oh, better I had floated with the stream,
Floated, and drowned among the muddy drift!"
Whereat the other clasps her in her arms,
And, speaking, smooths aside her tear-wet hair:
"We have been friends from childhood's early time,

When we went tottering truants to the field,
And lost ourselves among the harvest grass;
And we were friends together in the school,
Walking the path, at morn and eve, with hands
Locked each in each; and we were doubly friends,
When first we interchanged, in whispers low,
The secrets of our loves. And when misfortune
Falls, like a tree beneath whose shade we built,
Not dreaming of the storm, shall we not be,
As now we are, with triple friendship bound?
Look up, dear friend, and kiss me for reply.
E'en though an unkind father closed his door,
Another stands, inviting, open wide;
And when my Amy hath nowhere to rest,
Olivia shall be homeless. Cheer, take cheer!
The dreadful sea you shuddered to behold,
Is but a troubled verdure, like the prairie,
Which, from the distance, looks an ocean wide,
But nearer seen becomes a flowery pasture.
And look! the cloud, which threatened from afar,
Sails, like a ship, around the verge remote,
And leaves us undismayed!"

BOOK THIRTY-FIRST.

ONWARD still,
The giant movement goes with rapid pace,
And civilization spreads its arms abroad;
While the cleared forest-lands look gladly up,
And nod their harvest plumes. The summer speeds;
And many a whispering field of wheat and rye
Gleams, like a yellow sunshine, in the woods.
The grain, deep-standing, half conceals below
The primal roughness, where the reaper yet
Must take his difficult way; and there the maize,
With stalwart growth, as native to the soil,
Waves its tall martial tops, and gaily wears
Its tassel of soft silk. A few more days—
Behold the toilers lay their sickles by,
And all the sheaves are bound. Oh, happy time!
What season of the year so bright as this?

The labour done, the sultry crops are in,
And now they celebrate with harvest rites;
As in the dear and distant vales and years,
In shadowy ages of the Pagan past,
The "harvest home" was scene of sacrifice:
There the fat swine poured its red life away
Upon the altar stone; and, at the shrine
Sacred to Sylva, flowed the dairy flood.
To-day a kindred sacrifice is made;
But, with improved sense, the modern dame
Gives from her oven the well-garnished meat,
With crisped rind, and savoury with green;
And in great jars, fresh-dripping, icy-cool,
Cooled in the crystal at the shady spring,
The snow-white fluid gleams; where, not less white,
Is spread the crimped cloth beneath the trees,
O'er which the flecks of sun, on golden wings,
Flutter mid phantom leaves. The sports begin,—
The various games which please the rural mind,
And knit the manly frame. Some throw the ball;
From hand to hand the little messenger,
Swift as a meteor, flies. Beside the stream,
On plushy beds of greenest moss and grass,
The wrestlers ply the old Olympian game;
Struggling in friendly war, as struggled once—

So sings Jove's laureate—the heroes two,
Ajax and Ulysses, when Achilles
Bade the great game begin and end, and gave
To both, so equally they strove, the mead
Of well-earned victory. Through sun and shade,
Some in the foot-race emulate the deer;
Or, like the wild buck startled from his lair,
Leap the incredible space. While others bend
And lift the monster weight which, heaved beyond,
Deep dents the soil, and shakes the adjacent ground.
But, yonder, mark the sport which pleases most,
And most to be approved. Whirling in air,
The swift quoit cleaves its long and graceful arch,
And strikes, half-buried in the soil, aslant,
Beside the well-marked spot; on which a second,
With equal aim, oft clangs with fiery glance,
Flying aside mid shouts of those who win;
Or, with still nicer judgment sent, descends,
And crowns the difficult meg. Behold yon form
The moment when the balanced ring is sped—
The foot advanced—the expanded chest—the arm,
An instant stretched with open hand—the eye
Following the iron flight, e'en as an archer's
Chases his winged shaft! No nobler shape,
Or freer movement of the form divine,
May charm the artistic sight! So stands to-day

The sculptured Greek in Rome: as if great Jove,
Thrilling with admiration at the scene,
Had turned the man to marble when he threw,
And made the act immortal, that, henceforth,
The Parian shape should nobly teach the world
The manliest classic game. Far through the woods
Ramble fair bands of happy youths and maids;
And noisy children, curious in their search,
Proclaim the novel wonders where they go.
There blooms some unknown flower; and there hangs,
To ripen in the autumn frost, the wild
Banana of the North; and, lowly, there
The golden mandrakes, odorous, profuse,
Drag down their yellow stalks. Between the trees,
As through an antique colonnade o'ergrown
With moss and creeping vines, the lovers walk,
Musing, delighted, on the marvellous wild.
Here, gaze in wonder on the monster path
Where strode the great tornado, summers past,
O'erturning trees whose giant roots in air
Rose, like a barricade, behind its flight.
Or here, their light steps fright the astounded squirrel,
Which flies the prone logs to its native tree.
Behold these pillared trunks, which, ere they prop
Their rafter limbs, and cornice of deep green,
O'ertop the tallest oak in cultured fields;

Here Europe's groves might grow, and wave beneath,
Nor graze their plumes against the lowest branch:
Here hangs, as if from Heaven, the antique vine,
Or clasps the trunk with anacondian coils!
And where the younger festoon, like a rope
Drooping between two mast heads to the deck,
Sways in the wind, inviting to the young,
The woodland people, in their boisterous mirth,
Usurp the swing, and sweep the shadowy air.
Ye who condemn the red man's tameless life,
Go forth into the primal forest depth,
And feel the freedom which pervades its shade;
There taste the fruit upon uncultured stalks,
And slake your thirst at fountains, sunless, cool;
There note the game your every step shall start,
And you shall find, in your own Christian breast,
A savage spirit, pleading to remain,
Claiming its ancient patrimonial right.
    But hark, upon the breath of afternoon,
A sound is floating, and all stand to hear;
And e'en the birds sit listening in amaze;
In delicate notes, alternate heard and lost,
Breathed from the rosined cordage of the viol
It flows from out the clearing, and, at once,
All guess the call, and hasten to the scene,
Where dance and mirth fill up the fading hours.

BOOK THIRTY-SECOND.

Of all the lovely seasons of the year,
None is so full of majesty as this,
When red October, like a king of old—
As wise as rich, and generous as wise—
Smiles on the untaxed garners of the land.
The fields lie cleared and brown; and all the woods
Gleam with a mellow splendour, where the gold
Vies with the purple and the crimson glory,—
The sunset of the year. Whence soon shall follow
The gusty twilight of November days;
Then the dull, rainy eve, till Winter comes,
Like a white moonlight night, and shuts the scene
With his pervading snow. The prairie grass
Sways, seethes, and dryly rustles in the air—
A harvest sound, where only fire shall reap;
And over all an azure mist is spread,

Silent and dreamy, where the autumn sun
Rolls flushed and large; and, through the smoky sky,
The airy eagle, like a pirate bark,
Sails, tacks, and veers, and looks abroad for prey.
Now that the heavier tasks are done, the woods
Ring and re-echo, and the cabin walls
Are coated o'er with furry skins, to dry;
While oft the eve, beside the blazing fire,
Beholds the moulding of the murderous balls.
But, now, what means this early morning stir,
This general voice, and merriment abroad?
On restive steeds the assembled hunters mount;
The powder-oxhorn at each girdle hangs,
Swung like the forest-bugle worn of old.
Then weighs the laden pouch; and, in the belt,
The smaller fire-arms slant; while, in the hand,
The polished rifle gleams, and coils of rope
Hang at the saddle-bow,—a lasso rude.
And lo! the cavalcade across the stream
Dashes, with shouts, toward the prairie lands!
O'er the far plains, in dim and dusky lines,
Moving like wave on wave, their sight discerns,
Or fancies it discerns, the bison herd
Which roams the vernal sea; and, like a crew
That notes on the horizon, vague, remote,

Their giant prey, which spouts the brine in air,
And from the vessel drops, in venturous boats,
Striking abroad upon the billowy deep —
The pioneers sweep up against the wind,
Spreading as they approach, to circumvent,
That each may choose his victim from the flock,
And, as he passes, send the bolt of death.
Thus speed they on, with weapons grasped secure;
And near and near — more cautious as they near —
Widening the snary crescent of their line —
Till lo! the bearded patriarch of the herd
Exalts his front, and gives the quick alarm!
A sea of heads and horns is in the air;
And, swift as yesty waves before the gale,
Sweeps the full tribe, with their innumerous hoofs
Making continuous shudder in the ground,
Loud and tremendous, as when through the cane
Roars the tornado! Now the chase begins;
And, presently, the vollied rifles ring,
While here and there the dying monster drops;
Or, wounded, leaves behind the sanguine trail,
Till, fainter and more faint, he staggers, sinks,
While his pursuer tracks his flying mate.
Or see yon giant, where he stands at bay, —
The flashing eye-balls and the foaming mouth, —

The foam half crimson! From his fated side
The red stream pours, and still he bravely fronts
The assailing hunter, thrusting left and right,
And oft the wary charger, with his rider,
Darts from the plunging horns; and, as he fights,
He feels the numbing pain within his breast,
The leaden foe his fury cannot reach!
Still he resists; and slowly fails and fails—
His eyes grow filmy, and his sight is dim—
Sullen, from side to side, the great bulk sways—
The wide plain reels around him, and he falls,
And lifeless lies the hero of the herd!

What though the muse attempt the murderous scene,
Her spirit finds small pleasure in the song,
And shrinks before the vision she has drawn;
The sounds grate harshly, and seem out of tune,
Jarring against each other. Rather far
Her eye adventurous sweeps the distant hill,
And follows Arthur, where, with glittering hoofs,
His charger o'er the billows of the plain
Mounts and descends, to take the prairie-steed
Grazing among its fellows. The wild group,
With nostrils wide, soon note the scented air;
And o'er the ridge the unshod coursers speed,

Giving their streaming manes unto the wind,
Like that mad team which charioted the sun,
Flying afar, eccentric, unrestrained,
With Phaëton behind. In hot pursuit
The guided charger sweeps, and, taking oft
A shorter course direct, still intercepts;
And, straining every muscle, nears and nears,
Until the fatal cord is sped, and falls,
And the wild creature feels the tightening snare,
And yields at last unto the lariat curb;
Then, led in triumph to its captor's friends,
Stands with wide eyes of wonder. When the sun
Pitches his blazing camp along the west,
Following their lengthening shadows, stretching home,
The laden hunters ride; and in the dusk
Behold their fire-lit windows, like the stars,
Smile in the darkening east. The plain is past;
Their doors receive them; and throughout the eve,
Beside the autumn fire, sit gray-haired men,
And maids, and matrons, and the wondering young,
Listening the marvellous history of the day,
Where oft the shadowy people on the wall
Leap up, and clap their visionary hands.
Again the pictured bison toss away,
Shouldering o'er tangled grass—again the chase—

Again the bleeding giant fights and dies.
Musing and marvelling Master Ethan sits,
While on his chair Olivia leans, and hears
The glowing language which her lover breathes;
And when again the lariat takes the steed,
And the wild creature struggles with the noose,
Her wonder half to chastening pity melts.
So great the pleasure of the eventful time,
Each sighs to think of those, left far behind,
Who dream beside their tame ancestral hearths,
Dozing monotonous lives away, and longs
To pour into their ears the exciting theme,
And woo them to the West. Here, drawn apart,
Pale Amy listens, mourning in her soul,
Thinking of one who also, 'mong the rest,
Might have repeated to her charmed ear
The wild exploit; and, mid the smiles of all,
Returned the long-praised hero of the chase.
But hark, the song awakes the shadowy eve:

"Form the ring, and pile the fire;
Swell the chorus, like a choir,
While the minstrel wakes his lyre,
Bound with garlands never sere.

And, like holy stars arisen
From their orient blue prison,
Joy shall mount, and Peace shall listen,
While the social hearth shall glisten,
    On the newly-found frontier.

Let no dull regret remind us
Of the homes which lie behind us,
Or the tear of memory blind us
    To the world of beauty here:
Let the past retain its pleasure,
While the present, without measure,
Opes the promised land of treasure,
Where wide Freedom's dome of azure
    Overbinds the far frontier.

Soon the forest, like the bison,
Shall enrich the land it dies on,
And the ground, its shade now lies on,
    Smile in harvests broad and clear.
Then the gloom these lands inherit,
Like a shadow from the spirit
When the world rewards its merit,
Shall depart—the sun shall scare it—
    From the bountiful frontier.

Then, alone, within the furrow,
Or in woodland alleys narrow,
Shall some flint-head of the arrow
 Speak of tribes long sped from here;
Or the children, while they're playing,
Find the stone-axe in their straying,
Or the lone wigwam decaying—
The last fading signs betraying
 Who once ruled the dark frontier.

Round our barks yon stream shall ripple,
On our banks rise church and steeple,
Where the bell to busy people
 Shall ring, hourly, silver-clear.
And the eagle, sailing airy,
With his downward glances wary,
Shall behold the swift scene vary
Over forest, stream and prairie,
 Wondering at the changed frontier.

And his wings shall mount, affrighted,
O'er the scene so strangely lighted,
And to western wilds, benighted,
 Take his marvelling career;
Yet, before his flight he urges,
From the clearing's noisy verges,

He shall see the silvery surges
On the mill-wheel, hear the forges
    Which shall wake the far frontier.

And mid scenes of peaceful culture,
Shall the dove succeed the vulture,
E'er the pioneer's sepulture
    Tolls the bell or starts the tear.
And our State from its probation,
Soon shall take its glorious station
In the union of the nation,
And the coming generation
    Westward seek a new frontier."

The song is done. Lo, through the casement seen,
A marvellous light along the southern sky
Flames with an angry hue—as in the east,
Oft, o'er the full and yet unrisen moon,
The strange light blots through veils of evening-mist—
While, like an eagle's shadow, o'er the plain
The frequent deer flies north. The hungry wolf
Forgets his prey, and prowls into the woods;
The frighted steed, with many an unknown shape,
Sweeps past beneath the stars—as when at sea
The speeding tribes proclaim the foe behind.

And still the great light, on the prairie's verge,
Springs like the boreal glow in winter seen,—
A spectral, melancholy dawn: as if
The south would fling the north its splendours back;
Or earth, like some great vessel sideward thrown,
Had far careened, and from the tropics brought
The red, unnatural morn. And, thicker still,
Pour on the heterogeneous herds. And now
A roar sweeps wide upon the sultry air—
As when the wind, wet with Niagara's mist,
Bears the perpetual thunder leagues away—
It nears and nears. "The prairie is on fire!"
And the announcement flies from door to door,
Swift as from tent to tent a call to arms,
When down the distance pours the assailing foe—
"The prairie is on fire!" And on the wind
The red tornado spreads its blighting wings—
Fearful and splendid in magnificent rage—
Chasing the frantic dwellers of the plain,
Flying in reckless terror. Such the scene—
Abhorrent, awful, wonderful, sublime—
Which passed o'er Milton's inward sight, what time
He saw the infernal lake, when from the fire
The shadowy demons, to their master's call,
Sped in a cloud confused. Around the homes,

Pitched on the prairie's side, fear rules the scene;
And consternation throbs in every breast,
And stupifies the needed ready mind;
Till one, with cooler presence than the rest,
Grasps the great blazing brand, and wildly flies,
And streaks the grass with flame. The powdery mass
Flashes and roars; and, with its mane of fire,
Drives left and right; and, flickering to the skies,
Darts o'er the plain to west, and north, and south;
And, with the other merging, leaves the space
Where stand the anxious pioneers agaze,
While many a prayer of thankfulness ascends.

BOOK THIRTY-THIRD.

The skies are clouded, and the sad winds sweep,
Wailing along the forest, like a bard
Pouring a requiem upon his harp.
All sights and sounds are dreary; and the pipe,
So long attuned to pleasurable exploits,
Breathes like a widowed night-bird unconsoled.
A melancholy wide pervades the air
Whence falls the shadow? what invisible hand
Spreads the dusk veil? Is it that autumn drops
Her chilly mantle, like a funeral weed,
Trailing and rustling on the gusty wind?
Or some presentiment of ill to come,
Half comprehended, springs? Is it that grief
Stands ever at the chair of revelling joy,
To fill with bitter the alternate cup,—
A medicine to temper the sweet draughts

Which, else, would cloy and sicken? Let it pour!
It is the great Physician who prescribes!
Does disappointment lower? or yawns the grave?
Not even this should overcloud us so.
At all our portals death, impatient, stands;
As oft, beside the door of one who feasts,
The watchful bailiff waits. Who may escape?
We but prolong the banquet at the best;
And happy those who unbesotted rise,
With vision clear, and go to their account.
    O'er lands from which the driven savage flies,
A direful spirit lingers, as to avenge
The red man's wrongs,—to execute the curse
He breathed upon the landscape when he fled.
From lake and river, and low, sodden marsh,
The blighting phantom, on miasma's wings,
Rises, and sheds its night-brewed venom round;
And from its ghostly pinions widely fans
The alternate airs of dreadful fire and frost.
The incautious breast, inhaling unaware,
Now burns with heat, on winter's breath could quell;
Now shakes with cold, on furnace blast could reach;
Consuming now, as in a martyr's flame,
To shiver soon as in a cave of ice.
To grateful draughts now cling the fevered lips;

Now, pinched and purple, drain the scalding bowl:
Such is the startling blight the autumn sees
Sweep o'er the frontier homes. Here shuddering forth,
Seeking the sun against his cabin wall,
With trembly knees, the labourer, late so strong,
Now crawls to thaw the current of his blood,
Or shivers in the blazing chimney-side;
And there the matron droops. Crouched o'er the
hearth,
Baldwin, disheartened, gazes in the flame,
His sad soul aching with the internal cold.
Meanwhile, his good wife, struggling, unsubdued,
Holds, as with palsy-shaken arms, the child
Which, like an ember, burns upon her breast.
Olivia, only spared of all the house,
Glides, like an anxious angel, mid the group,
And fills her trebled duties all the day;
While frequent sunshine of her generous face
Gladdens the neighbouring doors. And Arthur oft,
Himself pursuing charitable paths,
Beholds her pass, and feels his love increase.
Nightly, by Amy's bed, her golden hair
Sheds a soft splendour; and her saint-like voice,
Low as the summer-music of a brook,
And mellow soul-light beaming from her eyes,

Half melt the ague from the sufferer's heart.
Here Master Ethan, ever on the alert,
Forgets himself, to go from couch to couch.
  Now, to the fevered fancy, glowing springs—
In all the brightness time and distance give,
When want and pain attend the exile's bed—
The charmed home, the dreamy-lighted vale,
The fire-side comforts, and the wholesome air;
Which once again to feel, and freely breathe,
Were panacea for the mind and frame
No subtle drug could match. Yet few there are,
In the heroic group, whose hearts, subdued,
Harbour the home-sick vision; but resist,
With stubborn valour, as a forest-tree
Resists the assailing blast. Beside the stream,
Where the low chapel lifts its modest head,
Of fresh-hewn timbers built, the first small mound
Is shaped; and Baldwin's household mourns. From there
The light of childhood passed; from out their door
The shape, so morning-halo d once, was borne,—
A little form of dull and sunless dust.
And now the rude inscription sanctifies
The enclosed spot, and to the future speaks:—
"The first pale flower here consecrates the ground."

Here Christmas comes—how different from the last!
The little stockings, at rude wooden jambs,
Are hung again with undiminished faith;
Each chest in secret turns its contents out,
And, ransacked oft, gives scantly to the time.
And meagre joy had crowned the prayed-for morn,
Had not Olivia's busy, generous hand
Oft plied the midnight needle, and, unseen,
Wrought curious shapes within the flowery tray;
While Arthur's dexterous knife, and ready taste,
Carved wooden forms of beautiful device.
The week, to happy childhood dear, departs.
Now sweeps the snow, and blows the boreal blast,
While winter, like a crabbed regent, rules
The young, obstreperous year. On many a night,
The wakeful household, shuddering with the wind—
Which searches every cranny, while the snow,
A powder fine, attends the inveterate gust—
Shall hear, dismayed, the direful panther's cry,
Startlingly human, and the adventurous wolf
Howling in fearful nearness; and, in dreams,
Behold the ravage wrought in bleating sheds!
And oft the pioneer shall start, alarmed,
And with the rifle steal into the dark

To guard the midnight fold. Such are the scenes,
The hardships, and the perils which deter
Full many a spirit in its eastern home,
Long wishing to be gone. The trials these
Which only sternest natures well can meet.
The fight is hard, the battle long sustained,
Ere the wild forest yields, and the broad land
With unresistance wears the peaceful yoke.
Bid civilization send unto her verge
The frame of iron and the heart of oak,
With courage, will and sinew to subdue:
Let gentler natures court a gentler scene.

BOOK THIRTY-FOURTH.

THE season comes when, from her three-month's trance,
The Earth awakes: already her deep heart
Begins to stir, and send its life abroad.
On slopes, which lie adjacent to the sun,
The snows grow thin and vanish, and the air
Is scented with the odours of the mould;
For there the Spring, with warm and delicate feet,
Fresh from her hidden caverns of perfume,
Walks in the noon to wake the early flowers.
Here the first bird begins the woodland's song;
But in yon maple grove, where genial airs
Are earliest to blow, and last to leave,
A louder voice is heard. The augur there
Passes from tree to tree, and deals the wound
Whence flows the saccharine crystal into troughs,
Propt at the great trunks' feet; while overhead

The squirrel swings, and looks in wonder down.
And now begins the pleasurable toil
Which tends the sugar camp. The fire is built:
All day the smoke rolls through the antique boughs,
All night the blaze illumes the forest-depths!
And there the giant cauldron seethes and steams,
Until the simple alchemy bestows
The dusky syrup which, in cooling jars,
Transmutes, and gives the granulated mass;
Or often, poured in shallow depths, contracts
To marble smoothness, waxen to the eye,
Hard to the tooth, delicious to the taste,
Dearer to childhood than a Christmas-toy.
It is the spring-time. Down yon woodland path
A lovely picture glides between the trees,
Taking its way unto the chapel-door.
Gay garments, and soft fluttering robes of white,
Charm the calm sunshine, while the swelling hymn
The slow procession chants, ascends the air,
And, unimpeded, passes into heaven.
Behold the pastor leads the sacred way,
Then Arthur and Olivia. Look again!
How beautiful the maiden's downcast eyes,
With drooping lids that hold the happy tears!
A hallowed dream-light floats o'er all her form;

The snowy vesture rustles at her feet,
With pleasant music, as of whispering leaves.
Her golden hair, the veil but half-way hides,
Sparkles with April's choicest violets,
By loving fingers plucked from sunniest spots,
While yet the morn was red. Her parents next,
Pale and disheartened with the trying year,
Follow, with Master Ethan at their side:
And not the memory of the long disease,
The want of comforts, and the weakening toil
Which their slow feet betray, can check the light
Of pleasure springing to their languid eyes.
And after these, upon her mother's arm,
Comes Amy, with weak trembling steps, her cheeks
Glowing, as fits the occasion; but, alas!
It is the fiery rose that fever gives,
Which, but a few hours hence, shall be consumed,
And leave the hue of ashes there instead!
Then follows the whole glad community;
And presently the sanctuary-door
Receives the line, and silence reigns without.
    Here while we rest, in quiet musing held,
And gaze upon the empty cabin-homes—
Where one stands waiting, with warm glowing arms,
For those we shall no more behold as two,

But bound together in that golden bond
Which, to the trusting heart, scarce death can break—
Let contemplation view the future scene.
    Afar the woods before the vision flies—
Swift as a shadow o'er the meadow grass
Chased by the sunshine—and a realm of farms
O'erspreads the country wide; where many a spire
Springs in the valleys, and on distant hills,—
The watch-towers of the land. Here quiet herds
Shall crop the ample pasture, and on slopes
Doze through the summer noon. While every beast
Which prowls, a terror to the frontier fold,
Shall only live in some remembered tale,
Told by Tradition in the lighted hall,
When the red grate usurps the wooded hearth.
Here shall the city spread its noisy streets,
And groaning steamers chafe along the wharves;
While hourly o'er the plain, with streaming plume,
Like a swift herald bringing news of peace,
The rattling train shall fly; and from the East—
E'en from the Atlantic to the new-found shores
Where far Pacific rolls, in storm or rest,
Washing his sands of gold—the arrowy track
Shall stretch its iron bond through all the land.
Then these interior plains shall be as they

Which hear the ocean roar. And northern lakes
Shall bear their produce, and return them wealth;
And Mississippi, father of the floods,
Perform their errands to the Mexic Gulf,
And send them back the tropic bales and fruits.
Then shall the generations musing here,
Dream of the troublous days before their time;
And antiquaries point the very spot
Where rose the first rude cabin, and the space
Where stood the forest-chapel with its graves,
And where the earliest marriage rites were said.
Here, in the middle of the nation's arms,
Perchance the mightiest inland mart shall spring.
Here the great statesman from the ranks of toil
May rise, with judgment clear, as strong as wise;
And, with a well-directed patriot-blow,
Reclinch the rivets in our union-bands,
Which tinkering knaves have striven to set ajar!
Here shall, perchance, the mighty bard be born,
With voice to sweep and thrill the nation's heart,
Like his own hand upon the corded harp.
His songs shall be as precious girths of gold,
Reaching through all the quarters of the land,
Inlaid so deep within the country's weal,
That they shall hold when heavier bands shall fail,

Eaten by rust, or broke by traitor blows.
Heaven speed his coming! he is needed now!
He wisely spake who said, "let me but sing
The songs, and let who will enact the laws."
There are whose lips are touched with living fire:
In this great moment are they silent now?
Lift up your foreheads, O, ye glorious few,
Exalt your laurels in the gusty air!
And, like brave heralds on a windy hill,
Let your clear voices as a bugle ring!
The wild time needs you. There are trembling hearts
To strengthen and assure; and there are tongues,
Uttering they know not what, that should be drowned,
And babbling lips that should be filled with song,
Lest they breathe treason unaware. Who dares,
Like that bad angel which dismembered Heaven,
Stand forth, and, with "disunion" on his lips,
Earn endless infamy? None are so base.
Or if he lives—the world on land and sea
Hides many monsters—let his villain tongue,
In its proclaiming, struck with palsy, cleave—
Cleave to the roof, as with a ten years drought,
And rot to ashes in the traitor's throat!
And may his arm which lifts the severing sword,
Be lightning-shivered ere it gives the blow!

And on his brow be branded these black words:
"Behold the Iscariot of his native land!"
Then drive him forth in all his impotence—
The wide earth's exile—an abhorred show!
O thou, my country, may the future on
Thy shape majestic stand supreme as now,
And every stain which mars thy starry robe,
In the white sun of truth, be bleached away!
Hold thy grand posture with unswerving mien,
Firm as a statue proud of its bright form,
Whose purity would daunt the vandal-hand
In fury raised to shatter! From thine eye
Let the clear light of freedom still dispread
The broad, unclouded, stationary noon!
Still with thy right hand on the fasces lean,
And with the other point the living source
Whence all thy glory comes; and where unseen,
But still all-seeing, the great patriot-souls,
Whose swords and wisdom left us thus enriched,
Look down and note how we fulfil our trust!
Still hold beneath thy fixed and sandal'd foot
The broken sceptre and the tyrant's gyves;
And let thy stature shine above the world,
A form of terror and of loveliness![6]

BOOK THIRTY-FIFTH.

ALONG yon rugged road which, like a stream,
Bursts through the shadowy forest to the west—
Where many a wain, like a deep-laden barge,
Sweeps with the current following the sun—
Behold to-day, with toilsome course reversed,
One lonesome team is heading to the east.
Crouched 'neath the cover, pale and sick at heart,
Like wounded sufferers from a camp of war,
The dwindled household of the pioneer
Pursues its homeward way. And when the wheel
Sinks, in the black mire stalled, 'tis Baldwin's arm,
Now robbed of half its strength, impels it on.
And Master Ethan on the prairie-steed,
The gift of Arthur, slowly rides beside.
Too stern the battle for such souls as theirs.
At best, the forest is a stubborn foe,

Debating every inch it gives; but when
His pale ally from sudden ambush springs,
And deals from unseen hands the certain blow,
They must be stout, indeed, who still resist,
Preferring death to honourable retreat.

When the third eve upon their labouring way
Threatens impending darkness, and the fire
Lights up their lone and ill-provided camp,
Which the red sunset mocks along the sky,
And the tired horses crop the scanty grass;—
Lo, to the wondering languor of their looks,
A dreary figure o'er the summit toils,
Approaching slowly; and the shadowy shape
Looms strangely dusk against the crimson west,
Startling in this lone place the sickly eyes
That watch the coming form. What may it be?
The shape is human; yet the clearings lie
So separated by long miles of woods,
To meet a lonely traveller in such place,
And at such hour, the coolest reason deems
The chance as rare; and fancy half believes
Yon nearing shade the nightly walking ghost
Of some poor pilgrim who, beside the road,
Sat down, wayworn, and laid its life-load by.
And still it nears, and still amazement springs.

Its robes disordered and o'erspread with mire—
Its wild hair floating—and its wilder eyes
Fearless and staring—and the parted lips
Breathing no audible sound—make it, indeed,
A sight to send a shudder through the soul,
And start the brow's cold dew. But hark, a cry
Of recognition thrills the twilight air,
And Amy's arms are round the matron's neck.
Oh, love, thy thorns outnumber all thy flowers;
And oft the frenzied eye-glance tells, as now,
How thy sharp, cheating garland wounds the brain!
Thy clearest streams oft wind to gulfs of wo—
Thy morning clouds of beauty end in storm—
Thy sheltering myrtles call the lightning down—
Thy violet by-ways tend to fields of briers—
Thy dove oft proves a vulture—and, in short,
So deeply art thou leagued with old despair,
Who sittest ever on a throne of tombs,
Thy brightest path leads nearest to his realm.
The heavy weeks toil past. June rules the sky.
When now, in middle of the afternoon,
The great white sun impends above the west,
Flooding the valley with his dreamy light—
Where farm, and village, and star-glittering spires
Shine like the enchanted realm of peace—behold,

On yonder brow beyond the crossing roads,
The little wagon rises, and stands still.
The weary horses droop; the harness hangs,
Along their lank sides, roughly and awry;
The careless rein drops, coiling, to the ground;
The dusty wain is loose and out of joint;
The cover soiled and warped. A dreary sight!
And not less woful, in their way-worn garbs,
The melancholy group whose tearful eyes
Take in the landscape dearest to their hearts.
And while they gaze, their joy is half rebuked
With wonder why they left so fair a spot.
Yonder, within its little knot of trees,
The sacred homestead smiles; and, there, the fields
Which called them to the harvest; but, alas,
The stranger in their native doorway stands,
His scythes along yon clover-pasture sweep,
And all the acres hold his waving crops.
The unknown mower wipes his reeking blade,
And, whistling, whets its sun-reflecting side;
The pleasant odour steals along the breeze,
Sweet as from out the hay-fields of the past;
The cow-boy, singing on the distant slope,
Turns home the tinkling herd. There springs the smoke

From long-remembered hearths. Some stranger smith
Awakes the ringing anvil; and from far,
The giant hammer of the stream-worked forge
Throbs through the air its old familiar beat.
There gleams the chapel on its Sabbath-hill,
Where now some foreign pastor wakes the desk;
And in the lowland, by the winding stream,
Flashes the mill-wheel; but who tends the mill?
Here, by the highway, the elm-shaded school
Lulls the soft air with murmurs; but within
What faithful master fills the sovereign chair?
Such are the sights and such the thoughts that rise,
Till each heart throbs with mingled joy and pain.
Their feet, forgetful of long travel past,
Receive new impulse, and descend the road,
Taking fresh vigour; as if e'en the dust,
Which held their footprints in their younger years,
Gave back the lightness of those brighter days.

So great a draft the westward-going line
Made on the happy vale, to fill the gap,
From various sides, came in the stranger crowd
Usurping fields and hearths. The homeward few
Gaze wistfully to meet one well-known face.
As yet but unfamiliar, curious looks,
Greet their return until their little wain

Drags its slow course toward the wayside inn,
The centre of the vale; when to their side,
With wondering eyes and questions on his lips,
One old-time friend, with many welcoming words
Assails the group, and guides it to his gate.
And there his good wife, with astonished tears,
Receives the way-worn pilgrims; while, outside,
The rattling bars admit the ungeared team.

BOOK THIRTY-SEVENTH.

THE red sun sinks, and brings the noiseless eve:
Within the orchard, ere he drops to rest,
The robin pours his vesper hymn—his voice
Closes the chorus of the day; while now,
Within the shadowy grove, the whip-poor-will
Takes up the song, and leads the nightly choir.

Through yonder lane one tall, frail figure moves—
Moves like a phantom, sighing where he goes—
While in the east the white moon, as in pity,
Watches his lingering steps. These are the fields
His once strong arm had cleared. In this same path—
Since when full half a century has flown—
He led his fair bride home. And these tall trees,
Whose high leaves whisper in the upper air,
He bore as saplings in his arms, and set
The roots, now spread so broad and deep. And here

His happy children played. But now, alas,
His feet intrude upon another's grounds;
And through yon garden, where the long-gone past
Oft heard his household singing mid the flowers,
The iron highway unrelenting cleaves—
Cleaves like an arrow through a heart forlorn—
Where soon the engine, with discordant wheels,
Shall scream and thunder by. He turns in pain,
And strides the new-mown fields—his fields no more—
And gains the little chapel. Its calm shape,
Unchanged, melts o'er his spirit like the smile
Of one whose tongue is ever tuned to peace;
And down the little garden of low tombs,
He walks once more among his cherished friends,
Brushing the dewy roses where they sleep.
Here feels at home—here breathes a freer air—
And in his deep heart hears the welcome given
Which strengthens and consoles. Long by one grave
He leans with tranquil tears; and stands as one
Who waits beside a happy palace-gate,
Hearing his comrade's gliding feet within,
And hearkens for the warder's opening key.
The warder lingers, but the feast will last;
And they who come to-morrow, and to-morrow,
Shall find the eternal banquet but begun.

With firmer steps the old man turns away—
Crosses the dewy pasture—threads the grove—
Till, at the woodland's edge, a sudden hand
Falls on his arm, and on his ear a voice
Familiar of the past: "This way, good friend,
For here is need of you!" And to her door
The dame of Oakland guides the willing feet.
"Step lightly and speak low!" and murmuring thus,
She leads across the time-worn sill. Her hand,
Palsied and shaking like a winter limb,
Points to the woful shape upon her couch.
"Behold, for thou art worthy to behold,
The frail form wrecked upon the reefs of wo!"
Whereat the other, sighing, deeply speaks:
"Good dame, 'tis well the healing arts are yours,
You know what plants may medicine her ills."
To which the crone:—"I know that sweet herd well;
Already she hath drained the bowl, and sleeps.
Believe me, friend, I am not wont to weep—
I thought my springs of pity all were dry—
And yet to-night mine eyes have known strange tears!
Speak low, she sleeps! Poor fool, I warned her oft!
Oh, double folly, thus to wander back,
To seek the thing which was not worth the finding!
But piteous Heaven, oft kinder than it seems,

Hath moved the wretch beyond her pure soul's reach.
A few days past, in some wild tavern brawl,
And 'mong companions fit, he made a boast—
The boast that only fools and liars make—
When scarce the words had passed his scoundrel lips,
One nobler than the rest, with sudden hand,
Dealt the red stroke that saved a maiden's honour!
The son proved worthy the bad-guiding sire,
Who, bloated like his swine, beside his still
Death slaughtered at a blow!—a hideous sight!
    Poor child, she sleeps! 'Tis but a half hour past
The hot delirium raged. A little while
She lay, and chided, with most piteous word,
The tardy lover; and, with broken sobs,
Told him the hardships of the lonely woods:
But even there, she said, were lovely spots,
And she had found them all—the rock, the glen,
And the deep sunless forest—charmed scenes,
Inviting all to love. Then, with a start,
And ghostly smile, like moonshine on her face,
She cried, 'Oh, mother, cease to chide! he comes!
I knew that he would come.' And darkly, then,
A sudden shadow passed across her brow;
And presently she whispered, 'Why so pale?
Why stands he there with such despairing eyes!

There's blood upon his forehead! there's a wound
Which only I should bind! Come, let me twine
This 'kerchief there! Oh, look not thus! smile once,
And I forgive!' Whereat she swooned, and slept
As she sleeps now!" "You mean the sleep of death!"
The old man cries, and starts unto the couch.
"What other sleep could soothe?" replies the dame;
"The slumber which we know is poor at best,
And full of night-mares!—but *her* dreams are past!"
And now the veteran takes the clay-cold hand,
Smoothes back the troubled tresses from her brow,
And sighs, "'tis well," and by the bedside prays.

When through the vale the melancholy news
Of their return is spread, the rural hearts—
For simple hearts lie openest to the touch—
Are waked to pity; and the gathered group,
The leaders of the place, consult, devise,
And settle the benevolent plan. And now,
A little home, with moderate acres round,
Receives the worthy farmer and his plow,
Where soon his household smiles with health renewed
The frail old Master, whose undimmed repute
Through many years had widened miles abroad,
Accepts the well-urged offer; and once more,
Content among the rosy girls and boys,

Resumes his morning and his evening walk.
His locks grow thinner, and his steps less firm,
But cheerily still he rules his small domain;
And e'en less frequent sounds his chiding voice,
While oft the unnoted fault goes by, and love
Out-rules the rusted rod. Behold, abroad
In summer-noon recess, what happier sight!
The glowing children with their laughter loud
Startle the scented air; and games begin,
Only to end what time the bell recalls.
How the glad foliage rustles overhead,
As if the angels hovered listening there,
Watching the innocent pastimes, likest that
In purity which cheers celestial groves!
The hour goes by, and still the urchins play;—
Another hour, and still another flies,
Until they deem a holiday is given.
And peering oft where, leaning on his desk,
The Master holds his wonted rest, they turn
And look with wonder in each other's eyes,
And then renew their games! Dear hearts, play on;
Your laughter cannot break his slumber now!
His hand of dust shall no more wake the bell;
A greater ruler hath dismissed the school;
The weary Master takes recess in Heaven!

The circling theme is clasped where it began;
But, lingering still within this happy vale,
The bard reluctant stands. The pipe, attuned
To melancholy, yet prolongs the sound,
Like waves that murmur when the breeze is done.
Ye who have followed in the long-drawn path,
And borne with patient steps your pilgrim-staffs,
Nor dropt aside, way-worn,—forgive the guide,
If oft, enamoured of the tune he played,
He vaguely wandered—like an April brook,
Blind and oblivious, on its singing way—
And led through tedious woods and briery fields;
And, like brave travellers from a various tour,
Forget the toil—the dull, inclement days—
Recalling only landscapes bright with sun.

THE END.

NOTES.

Page 26.

[1] All week he tends within his noisy mill.

There are those who, perhaps, will be struck with the novelty of a man devoting his Sabbaths to the pulpit, and his week-days to an occupation which would seem to allow him but little time for study and meditation; but if they knew our rural districts better, they would probably call to mind many originals of the picture which I have attempted to draw. The "local preacher," I believe, not only receives no salary, but is generally one of the first persons called upon in cases of charity. It is with no intention to disparage the ministerial profession that this character is drawn; on the contrary, no one can hold in higher esteem than I do, that valorous army of ill-rewarded men who nobly sacrifice all worldly considerations for the amelioration of their fellows.

Page 59.

[2] The king-bird hovers, darting on his prey,
And takes the ventured argosy of sweets.

Since this passage was written, the supposed fact has become a disputed question. I shall be glad to find that I have done this little marauder injustice.

Page 116.

> [3] And much they talk
> Of news which, lately, from the far-off West,
> Startled the calm community.

The time represented in this poem, was about the year 1832, at which period, as many will remember, the "backwoods fever" was especially prevalent.

Page 185.

> [4] Such was the realm of Boone, the pioneer,
> Whose statue, in the eternal niche of Fame,
> Leans on his gleaming rifle.

If it is not taking too much liberty, I would suggest that Kentucky might also find a niche in her capitol for a statue of the father of her state. It is a subject which her own sculpter, Mr. Hart, would treat with propriety and enthusiasm.

Page 191.

> [5] Thou, who beneath thine own Catawba vine.

There is no man to whom the West is more indebted than to Mr. N. Longworth, of Cincinnati. And chief among the benefits which he has conferred must be regarded the introduction of the grape-culture. The country will yet acknowledge him to be the most effectual apostle of Temperance: for it is a remarkable fact, that the vineyard is the antagonist of the still-house, and that in vine-growing countries the curse of alcohol is not known.

Page 236.

> [6] And let thy stature shine above the world
> A form of terror and of loveliness.

This passage was suggested by Powers' statue of "America,"—one of the few works worthy to become the property of a nation.

www.ingramcontent.com/pod-product-compliance
Lightning Source LLC
LaVergne TN
LVHW010255110826
845151LV00004B/1481
9781425522568